VISION FROM THE HILL

The Historical Series of the Reformed Church
in America

No. 12

VISION FROM THE HILL

Selections from Works of Faculty & Alumni,
published on the Bicentennial of the
New Brunswick Theological Seminary

Edited by
John W. Beardslee III

Wm. B. Eerdmans Publishing Co.
Grand Rapids, Michigan

Grateful acknowledgement is made of permission to reprint the following copyrighted material:

"War Is the Enemy," from *The Essays of A. J. Muste*, copyright 1967 by A. J. Muste, used with permission of the publisher, Bobbs-Merrill, Inc.

"We Are Ambassadors" and "The Protestant Witness," from *Preaching Unashamed*, by Joseph R. Sizoo, used with permission of the copyright owner, the Abingdon Press.

Library of Congress Cataloging in Publication Data
Main entry under title:

Beardslee, John W. III, 1914-
   Vision from the hill.

  (The Historical series of the Reformed Church in
America; no. 12)
   1. Theology—Addresses, essays, lectures. 2. New
Brunswick Theological Seminary. I. Beardslee, John W.,
1914-   . II. New Brunswick Theological Seminary.
III. Series.
BR50.V556   1984   230'.5732   84-8137
ISBN 0-8028-0035-1

Contents

The Historical Series of the Reformed Church in America

This series has been inaugurated by the General Synod of the Reformed Church in America, acting through its Commission on History, for the purpose of encouraging historical research and providing a medium wherein this knowledge may be shared with the academic community and with the members of the denomination in order that a knowledge of the past may contribute to right action in the present.

It is an especial pleasure to present to the church this volume to celebrate the bicentennial of New Brunswick Theological Seminary in the Year of our Lord 1984.

General Editor

The Rev. Donald J. Bruggink, Ph.D., Western Theological Seminary

Preface

The Bicentennial Committee of the New Brunswick Theological Seminary asked a publications committee to prepare a collection of writings by faculty and alumni of the seminary to illustrate its history during the two hundred years of its witness.

The committee, composed of Herman Harmelink III (1958), Raymond J. Pontier (1941), Norman E. Thomas (1944), Charles J. Wissink, and John W. Beardslee III (chair), has worked often by correspondence and individual consultation, but all members have contributed significantly to the result. Special recognition goes to Herman Harmelink for writing the introduction. Charles Wissink suggested some of the themes that might give order and continuity to the work. The drudgery of proofreading has been lightened by the assistance of David Armstrong and Marsha Hoffman. The individual headings on the separate writings are the work of the chairperson, who has made a number of arbitrary decisions and bears the responsibility for the failings of the work.

In the preparation of the volume, it was understood that no writing by persons now living would be included, and that no attempt would be made, by modernization or otherwise, to secure uniformity in style. In every selection, therefore, paragraphing, punctuation, spelling, and capitalization follow the original printed work, except where an obvious error was found. This procedure contributes an authentic historical flavor to the work.

The title of the volume is the one suggested by Mrs. Carol Kinsey of the staff of the Gardner A. Sage Library.

John W. Beardslee III
New Brunswick Theological Seminary

Foreword

The 200th anniversary of America's oldest theological seminary, New Brunswick, provides the occasion for both a history of the seminary (written by its president, Dr. Howard G. Hageman), and a selection of writings published by faculty and alumni of the seminary. Dr. John W. Beardslee III, professor of church history at New Brunswick, chaired the committee making the selections, which concentrate on the themes of mission, unity and social action. These selections give an impression of the thinking and the concerns of New Brunswick men through two centuries.

New Brunswick's life begins with the election of John Henry Livingston as professor of theology by the General Synod of the Reformed (Dutch) Church in America in 1784, while he was minister of the Collegiate Church in Manhattan. His role in reuniting the two factions of the Dutch Reformed Church in the previous decade made him a suitable choice in founding theological education for the denomination. His theology reflects Dutch and Continental pietism, colored by a distinctively American experience, and rapidly becoming an assimilated part of American Christianity. His thinking was not bound by any narrow confessionalism, as is evidenced by his work in founding a school (Erasmus Hall, Brooklyn) named for the great Dutch humanist, but no serious problems with the orthodoxy of Dort were recognized. That orthodoxy was quietly assumed and expounded along with new interests.

The most important of these new interests was Protestantism's transforming experience of the century—the missionary movement, and that is the aspect of Livingston's career included here. *The Everlasting Gospel*, one of his two great published missionary sermons, resulted from his enthusiastic participation in the movement's early phase, and had a profound influence on the life of Samuel Mills and other pioneers. Faults in its biblical interpretation and historical assumptions are easy to find now, but the vision and hope are clear, and the impact of the Book of Revelation, when taken as a summons to Christian living rather than as an intellectual puzzle, is both striking and exemplary.

This missionary movement is one strand of Christian discipleship which marked the seminary from the beginning, waxing and waning at various times but always forming part of the life-giving environment of the school. Commitment to world mission, beginning with interdenominational missionary societies, deeply affected the spiritual life of the seminary, as can be seen in James Cannon's concept of the pastoral prayer. It also played a major role in one of the seminary's outstanding features—its abiding concern for ecumenical relations within the Christian family and its interest in cross-cultural contacts in mission. Samuel Zwemer, one of its greatest missionaries, did much of his best work in other denominations; his contemporary, Horace Underwood, left the Reformed Church on graduation to become a Presbyterian pioneer in Korea; A.L. Warnshuis devoted much of his lifetime of service to an ecumenical agency, the International Missionary Council. More recently the seminary has continued to see a number of its graduates serve as "foreign missionaries" under non-Reformed Church, but usually ecumenical, auspices.

The selections included in the present volume are mere introductions to the richness of this heritage. The century-long missionary spirit was kept alive by the typically American form of pietism, an individualistic gospel which stressed both the depth of human depravity and the need for personal rebirth. Revivalistic methods which played such a large part in American church growth in the 19th century caused concern to Cannon, McClelland and Berg—conservative Reformed churchmen who held reservations about such methods, in spite of praise sometimes given T.J. Frelinghuysen, who had used similar methods a century earlier. The "new methods" associated with Charles G. Finney—anxious meetings, emotionalism, etc.—were resisted by New Brunswick men in a reflection of the older Calvinism, which feared Arminianism and every form of reliance on human achievement. Solomon Froeligh, Livingston's erstwhile colleague who led the 1822 schism resulting in the True Reformed Dutch Church, had through his criticism of any doctrine smacking of "unlimited atonement" cast his shadow over the debate about encouraging the unregenerate to use the means of grace. McClelland shows that he learned from the world as well as from the old textbooks; his firm adherence to experience keeps his orthodoxy realistic.

Toward the mid-nineteenth century the scholasticism of Dort was wearing thin, but no substitute for it was acceptable. The German Reformed Mercersburg theology, with its effort to think historically about the Scriptures and the church's history, encountered resistance. Just as the secular nativists and "know-nothings" espoused a traditional anti-Romanism, so in the church Professor Berg, who now left the German Reformed Church for New Brunswick, gave the seminary a special tone as defender of the old, frightened orthodoxy, unhistorical and unwilling to learn from the world. Even Berg's appreciation for the irenic features of the Heidelberg Catechism failed to produce any hope for Christian growth apart from a rigid upholding of the old forms.

The literalism produced by the "Berg spirit" was akin to that of Old School Presbyterians, at Union Seminary but more emphatically at Princeton, with Alexander, Hodge and Warfield giving American scholastic Calvinism its great native expression. For nearly half a century (1857-1901), Professor Samuel Woodbridge, class of 1841, represented this type of theology at New Brunswick. His *Outlines of Systematic Theology*, used in translation also in India and Japan, are not represented in this collection because its teachings are more adequately found in the pages of his Princeton contemporary, Charles Hodge. This scholastic orthodoxy passed from complacency into crisis and wore itself out in the early twentieth century in fundamentalist-modernist controversies, most notably at Princeton.

New Brunswick was, by and large, spared such controversy by worthy representatives of a different and more open spirit, ready to learn from the world in the spirit of McClelland, at work parallel to the Berg-Woodbridge tradition. This is the period both of great missionaries and of exciting new lines of ministry which recognized new resources as well as new problems. Talmage's recognition of social responsibility in connection with China's opium problem, a fruit of European-American imperialism, was one of the forerunners of an evolving Christian social conscience. Two giants, Graham Taylor and A. J. Muste, made their contributions in service through other denominations, and are represented here by works of their later years. Faculty member John De Witt, whose *What Is Inspiration?* is the most significant piece of theological writing in its time produced in this seminary, represented the breakthrough of the new biblical criticism, throwing off the outmoded doctrinaire approaches of the past. He, along with colleague John Lansing, served in the preparation of the American Standard Version of the Bible, and gave New Brunswick a long period of distinguished biblical scholarship. Ferdinand S. Schenck, at the beginning of the present century, wrote forthrightly and progressively on a number of important topics— social responsibility and evolutionary thought among them—which pointed to a future in the main line of American Protestantism, and which make so much current fundamentalist obscurantism seem utterly outdated.

This main line of Protestantism was disturbed by fundamentalist agitation and new ideas just at the time, in the second quarter of the century, that the Reformed Church's sense of identity was damaged by misunderstandings between the old East and the growing, Western section of the church, immigrant based and held together by ethnic cohesiveness and a pietism which survived in a rural environment. Under the careful leadership of presidents William H. S. Demarest and John W. Beardslee, Jr., the seminary tried to remain in communication with the West, but often found its leading ideas branded as liberal. The inaugural addresses of professors two decades apart, Worcester and MacLean, were both attacked for historical-critical positions which would now be generally accepted in most parts of the church. This scrupulosity and negative scrutiny of new or unfamiliar ideas on the part of the West undoubtedly helped to stifle creative theological writing in the mid-twentieth century. Published writing is of course only one index of institutional life, and New Brunswick continued to have its great teachers, its pastoral administrators and its able leaders. Through the decades of controversy New Brunswick survived by providing strong leadership for the pastoral ministry, and the words to the preacher by that great preacher, Dr. Sizoo, alumnus and former president, form a timely conclusion addressed to the seminary's task of preparing its graduates for the ministry of Word and Sacrament into its third century.

                                                        Herman Harmelink III

I

John Henry Livingston, 1746-1825

Dr. Livingston was professor of theology from 1784 until his death, serving first in New York and Brooklyn in combination with his pastoral duties in the Collegiate Church and responsibilities in connection with the Erasmus Hall academy, and later in New Brunswick in connection with his presidency of Queen's College. Among his other interests one of the most fruitful was the emerging foreign missionary movement, to which he devoted much of his energy, and on whose behalf he preached this famous sermon, "The Everlasting Gospel," in 1804, while still serving in New York.

The Everlasting Gospel

REVELATION xiv. 6, 7.

AND I SAW ANOTHER ANGEL FLY IN THE MIDST OF HEAVEN, HAVING
THE EVERLASTING GOSPEL TO PREACH UNTO THEM THAT DWELL
ON THE EARTH, AND TO EVERY NATION, AND KINDRED, AND TONGUE,
AND PEOPLE, SAYING, WITH A LOUD VOICE, FEAR GOD, AND GIVE
GLORY TO HIM; FOR THE HOUR OF HIS JUDGMENT IS COME: AND
WORSHIP HIM THAT MADE HEAVEN, AND EARTH, AND THE SEA, AND
THE FOUNTAINS OF WATERS.

THE glory of God, the love of Christ, and the salvation of sinners,
suggest constraining motives for propagating the Gospel. The command
to *teach all nations,* and the promise that the word shall *not return
void,* present a warrant and encouragement to vigorous exertions for
converting the heathen. Christians have always recognized the obliga-
tion, and professed a submission to this duty; yet they have criminally
neglected the means, or ignobly slumbered in the work.

In the dark period of ignorance and oppression, when the Church
fled before an implacable enemy, it was impossible to devise liberal
plans, or prosecute any benevolent design for the enlargement of the
Redeemer's kingdom. Her situation precluded every generous effort.
But why, in more prosperous times, did believers abate in their zeal?
Why, for the space of centuries, when placed beyond the reach of persecution, have no strenuous measures been adopted for extending the
knowledge of the Saviour? Men, eminent for their piety and talents,
have, in succession, been raised up in the Church. Many, during this
long interval, have defended the truth, and, by their invaluable writings, recommended the excellence and power of godliness. Faithful and
learned ministers have indefatigably laboured; and the Lord hath often
sent a plentiful rain, and confirmed *his inheritance when it was weary:*
but still an extensive promulgation of the Gospel has not been seriously
attempted. Nothing since the primitive ages of Christianity, deserving
the name, has appeared, until the present period. Now, at a season the
most unpromising, when wars, revolutions, and confusion prevail; now,
when infidelity assumes a formidable aspect, increases its votaries, and
arrogantly threatens to crush revealed religion; at this very time, under

2

all these inauspicious circumstances, see the Church *enlarging the place of her tent, and stretching forth the curtains of her habitation! She breaks forth on the right hand and on the left, to inherit the Gentiles, and make the desolate cities to be inhabited.* All who embrace the doctrines of grace, in every nation, seem inspired with the same spirit. Vast plans are formed, immense expenses incurred, and the most distant continents and islands become the objects of attention. Now, the deplorable state of those who *dwell in the land of the shadow of death,* and perish for lack of knowledge, excites compassion. Societies are instituted to facilitate the work; and men, zealous and intrepid in the service of their Lord, readily offer to visit the uttermost ends of the earth, and cheerfully submit to the toils and dangers inseparable from missionary labours.

Such views and efforts constitute a distinguished epoch in the history of the Church. Events so singular, and in their consequences so interesting, create serious inquiries. The assiduous observer of Divine Providence, losing sight of subordinate agents, looks up, and asks, What is God doing? Why are the intricate wheels, which, with respect to this important object, have so long seemed stationary, now put in motion? Is there nothing in the word of God, is there no promise, no prediction, which will illustrate the procedure of Providence, and inform his people of the rise and progress, the source and tendency of this astonishing movement? From the prophecies of the Old Testament respecting the kingdom of Christ, a satisfactory reply cannot be obtained. Those prophecies refer chiefly to the beginning or to the conclusion of the Gospel dispensation. Some were accomplished in the days of the apostles and their immediate successors. The most of them look forward to a distant period. Very little concerning the intermediate space, or the train of events which mark the approach, and are to usher in the glory of the latter days, can be from them expressly collected. Our blessed Lord, in many of his parables, delineates the gradual and extensive progress of his kingdom. In the Epistles a formidable adversary is mentioned, *whom the Lord shall consume with the breath of his mouth, and shall destroy with the brightness of his coming.* But our most decisive information is to be derived from the APOCALYPSE. The various vicissitudes which, in succession, designate the present dispensation of the Church, and the time when the promises will be fulfilled, are there more pointedly described than in any other portion of the sacred scriptures. To a prophecy in this book I have presumed, my Brethren, upon this occasion, to request your attention:—a prophecy in which you will find an answer to your inquiries, and from which it is my design to deduce a NEW

MOTIVE for strenuous and persevering exertions in your missionary engagements.

Convinced of the difficulties which unavoidably attend the explanation of prophecies not yet accomplished, and persuaded of a prevailing disposition to magnify present events; aware of the propensity which urges to anticipate what is future, and sensible of the peculiar circumspection with which we ought to comment upon the book of Revelation; I approach my subject with humility and diffidence; yet not without hope that the meaning of the Holy Spirit, in the passage selected for our meditation, is rightly apprehended, and that something may be adduced for instruction and edification. Let us endeavour,

I. To ascertain the object of this prophecy; and then,

II. Investigate the period of its accomplishment.

First. To ascertain the object of this prophecy, and determine what event is here predicted, let it be observed, that in this chapter several distinct visions are recorded, which follow each other in uninterrupted succession, referring to events which, in that very order, will be accomplished; that the vision now under consideration is the second, and, in regard to its meaning and precise object, is uninfluenced by what precedes or follows.

John once *beheld and heard an angel flying through the midst of heaven, saying, with a loud voice, Woe, woe, woe to the inhabiters of the earth!* The characters and scene now before us are of a different nature: instead of woe and alarm, they are replete with glad tidings and consolation. I SAW ANOTHER ANGEL FLY IN THE MIDST OF HEAVEN, HAVING THE EVERLASTING GOSPEL TO PREACH UNTO THEM THAT DWELL ON THE EARTH. In this text the *hieroglyphical* and *alphabetical* language both occur. A few symbols are first introduced, after which an explanation succeeds in the ordinary style.

The symbols are, *heaven*, and an *angel*, bearing a precious treasure, *flying in the midst of heaven*, and crying with a *loud voice*. HEAVEN is often, throughout the scripture, used literally to indicate the place of glory, the beatific vision, the mansion of the blessed. In the passage before us it is a symbol, and means the Church under the New Testament dispensation. The *midst of heaven*, then, is the midst of the Christian Churches. ANGEL is an official term: it is frequently applied to those spiritual and celestial beings who are sent forth to minister to the heirs of salvation; but the word expresses not so much the nature as the character and duty of those who are employed as messengers. It is here a symbol, and represents the ministers of the Gospel, the messengers of the Lord to his people; and means not one particular minister, but a Gospel ministry in the aggregate. Of this a satisfactory explanation occurs in the second and third chapters of this book, where the symbol always refers to the ministry of the Churches. FLYING is the figure of speed. A continued flying indicates an uninterrupted and unceasing progress. The LOUD VOICE expresses earnestness, zeal, and authority.

From the symbolical terms we then collect, that John foresaw a period when a zealous ministry would arise in the midst of the Churches, with a new and extraordinary spirit; a ministry singular in its views and exertions, and remarkable for its plans and success; a ministry which would arrest the public attention, and be a prelude to momentous changes in the Church and in the world.

The LITERAL explanation removes every doubt respecting the meaning of these symbols. What is the treasure the angel bears? What does he proclaim with so loud a voice? To whom is his message directed? Each of these is here determined. The angel has the everlasting Gospel to preach: this is his treasure. He calls to the practice of the essential duties of true religion, and announces the hour of God's judgment: this is the import of his proclamation. He is commissioned to visit every nation and people on the earth: to them his message is directed.—Some of these articles deserve a minute discussion; but we must be contented with a few brief observations upon each.

1. The GOSPEL signifies good tidings, tidings of great joy, of salvation for lost sinners, salvation from great misery, procured by a great price, a great salvation. To PREACH this Gospel is officially to declare the fact, and authoritatively to command and persuade sinners to be reconciled to God. So the celestial angel preached the Gospel to the shepherds in the field of Bethlehem, when he published the birth of the Saviour. So the apostolic angels preached the Gospel when they went forth *as ambassadors for Christ*, and inculcated repentance and faith. So the ordinary angels of the Churches have continued in every age to preach the Gospel, as far as they have faithfully professed and taught the doctrines of Jesus and his apostles.

This Gospel is here called EVERLASTING, not merely because it was devised in the eternal counsel of peace between the Father and the Son, and because it is established by an everlasting covenant, which renders all the benefits well ordered, sure, and perpetual: but it is thus denominated, with particular emphasis, in this prophecy, to indicate that the Gospel, which should go forth from the midst of the Churches, and be sent to all the nations of the earth, would be the *same* Gospel which had always been maintained by the faithful followers of the Redeemer; the same Gospel which was *preached before unto Abraham;* the same which all believers embraced under the Old Testament; the same which the Apostles preached and the primitive Christians professed; the same to which the sealed of the Lord bore witness during the persecution of antichrist; the same for which the Churches at the Reformation protested, and which has since, by many of those Churches, been preserved in its purity. The very same weapons, and no other, which had been *mighty through God to the pulling down of strong holds* heretofore, should now be effectually employed. This ascertains that, at the period intended in the vision, the doctrines of grace would be faithfully preached; that the missionaries sent out from the midst of the Churches would be, like Barnabas, *good men, full of the Holy Ghost and of faith;* that they would not accommodate their message to the pride of philosophers, to the prejudice of infidels, or the bigotry of idolaters; but honestly, plainly, and boldly preach *Christ, and him crucified;* Christ, *the way, the truth, and the life,* by whom alone sinners can come to the Father, that, without flattery or disguise, they would call transgressors to repentance, and offer a Saviour to the chief of sinners.

2. To what doth the angel call? What is the import of his proclamation? In three comprehensive sentences a summary of the whole is exhibited—*Fear God; give glory to him;* and *worship him.* By the FEAR of God, the whole of true religion, as it respects principles and practice, is often expressed; particularly a veneration for the infinite majesty of Jehovah, and a holy dread of his judgments. *The Lord is the true God, he is the living God, and an everlasting King; at his wrath the earth shall tremble. Who would not fear thee, O King of Nations? for to thee doth it appertain.* But the fear particularly inculcated by the Gospel is here especially intended; not a servile dread, which urges awakened sinners to despair, and extinguishes devotion; but a holy reverence, blended with such perfect love as casteth out slavish fear. The spirit of adoption seals the forgiveness of sins—is an earnest of acceptance *in the beloved*—and excites in his people a filial fear. *There is forgiveness with thee, that thou mayest be feared.*

GIVE GLORY TO HIM, is added by the angel, as another comprehensive summary of the Gospel call. In all his divine attributes God is infinitely glorious. The heavens declare his glory. The whole earth is full of his glory. All his works praise him. He is glorious in his holiness and fearful in his praises. But in the face of Jesus Christ the glory of God shines most conspicuously. In the salvation of guilty, depraved, and helpless transgressors, through the imputed righteousness of the blessed Immanuel, glory redounds to God in the highest. The Gospel displays *the glory of his majesty;* and wherever it is rendered the wisdom and power of God unto salvation, it instructs the redeemed to *give glory unto the Lord.*

The angel concludes with the authoritative command, WORSHIP HIM. Revealed religion restores true worship to the world, directs to the right object, and opens the only way for sinners to the mercy-seat. It is with peculiar propriety the prophecy mentions, that the worship taught by the Gospel is the worship of the Creator, who MADE HEAVEN, AND EARTH, AND THE SEA, AND THE FOUNTAINS OF WATERS. It inculcates this great truth, that revealed religion adopts, confirms, and enjoins the religion of nature; that God, who is related to us as CREATOR, has revealed himself also in the new and adorable relation of REDEEMER; that sinners, therefore, who come to the Saviour, come to him who made them: in worshipping their Redeemer they worship their Creator. *Thy Maker is thy husband.*

This meets the objections of infidelity, and seems to point to prevailing principles at the time when the event foretold will be accomplished. The everlasting Gospel which the angel proclaims demonstrates the religion of nature, however perfect in itself, to be inadequate for the salvation of those who have sinned. It declares the Creator to be a Redeemer, and in this relation invites sinners to fear God, to give him glory, and worship him.

As a motive for preaching the Gospel, and an argument for its reception, the angel announces that THE HOUR OF GOD'S JUDGMENT IS COME. The term *judgment*, in the Apocalypse, usually respects the decision of the controversy which has long subsisted between the world and Jesus Christ; but it is evident a particular reference is here made to the judgment to be inflicted upon the nations chargeable with slaying the witnesses. *The nations were angry, and thy wrath is come, and the time of the dead that they should be judged;* the time when the dead saints shall be remembered, and the blood of the martyrs, by terrible judgments, be avenged. This is considered as the commencement of that awful decision, the beginning of that series of judgments, which will terminate the controversy between the Redeemer and his adversaries. To this, in the first instance, the angel has respect. He calls with *a loud voice—the hour of his judgment is come.* Let the nations tremble; let the world adore; especially let the Churches hear! The beginning of this judgment, the very hour of its commencement, is the signal for the angel's flight, and for extending the Redeemer's kingdom.

3. To whom is the Gospel to be sent? To whom is the angel commissioned to carry his treasure? UNTO THEM THAT DWELL ON THE EARTH, AND TO EVERY NATION, AND KINDRED, AND TONGUE, AND PEOPLE. The term EARTH, when used figuratively in this book, is a symbol for the Roman Empire, including the whole extent of the papal hierarchy. Commentators, who view it here as a symbol, understand the

prophecy as only foretelling the promulgation of the Gospel in its purity, throughout the bounds of that empire, as it is now divided into different nations, tongues and people. But the term has a literal meaning, and occurs here in connection with the alphabetical language: it must, therefore, be understood in its literal sense, indicating the whole globe which we inhabit, with all the nations and people of the world. To these, however distant and dispersed, diversified in their situation, and differing in their manners and languages; to all these the angel bends his course; to all these he is commissioned to preach the everlasting Gospel.

You have the meaning of the prophecy. What was suggested by the hieroglyphic, is illustrated and confirmed by the alphabetical language.

John saw in vision, that after a lapse of time, a singular movement would commence, not in a solitary corner, but in the very midst of the Churches—That the Gospel, in its purity, would be sent to the most distant lands, and success crown the benevolent work. The ordinary exercise of the ministry, or the feeble attempts which, at different times, might be made to propagate the Gospel, were not the object of this vision. It was something beyond the common standard, which the apostle beheld with admiration and rapture. It was such preaching and such propagation of the Gospel as John never before contemplated. There was a magnitude in the plan, a concurrence of sentiment, a speed in the execution, a zeal in the efforts, and a prosperity in the enterprize, which distinguished this from all former periods.

The event here described comprehends a series of causes and effects, a succession of means and ends, not to be completed in a day, or finished by a single exertion. It is represented as a growing and permanent work. It commences from small beginnings in the midst of the Churches, but it proceeds, and will increase in going. There are no limits to the progress of the angel. From the time he begins to fly and preach, he will continue to fly and preach until he has brought the everlasting Gospel to all nations, and tongues, and kindred, and people in the earth. Hail, happy period! hail, cheering prospect! When will that blessed hour arrive? When will the angel commence his flight? This leads us,

Secondly. To investigate the time when this prophecy will *begin* to be accomplished.

The whole structure of the vision, the grandeur of the scene, and the solemn exposition of the symbols, recommend this illustrious prophecy to the peculiar notice of the Churches; and yet it seems to have been generally neglected or misrepresented by commentators. It has either been restricted to what happened at the Reformation, or thrown into the great mass of events which are to take place after the Millennium has fully commenced. Whereas, upon examination, it will be found, both from the order of the vision, and its express object, that it comprehends something vastly beyond what was realized at the Reformation. And, so far from actually belonging to the millennial period, it is only the appointed *means* for introducing that state; whatever may be its progress or consummation, it must, in the nature of things, *begin* its operation some considerable time before the Millennium *can* commence. Let us impartially examine the subject.

Prophecy is furnished, like history, with a chronological calendar; and the predictions, with respect to the time of their accomplishment, may be referred to three distinct classes. *Some* expressly specify the period when the thing foretold shall take place, and give, either in literal or symbolical numbers, the exact series of years that shall elapse before the fulfilment. So to Abraham it was said in plain terms, that four hundred years should pass away before his posterity would be freed from bondage. So seventy years were appointed for Judah to remain in captivity. So also seventy weeks, a symbolical term for four hundred and ninety years, were to intervene between the decree of Artaxerxes and the death of the Messiah. *Other* predictions do not specify any series of years from which a computation can proceed, but connect the event with something preceding or subsequent. In such, the key of explanation must be found in the *order* of the events. To the *third* class belong those prophecies in which no time is mentioned, and no order established, but other events are predicted, and declared to be co-existent. Whenever, therefore, those take place, the event in question may be expected.

Agreeably to this arrangement, we find the prediction now under consideration does not belong to the *first* class. There is no mention of time, no period named, no number of years, either symbolical or literal, from which a calculation can proceed, or any expectation be formed, when the preaching angel will begin his flight.

To the *second* class it must be attached. To the *order* of the event we must be principally indebted for information. The vision before us is the second recorded in this chapter. Consistently with an established rule respecting an uninterrupted order of prophecies expressing the *actual series* of events, the time when the angel will commence his preaching must be, after what is intended by the first vision, and before the third. At some period between these two extremes this prophecy will be accomplished.

What was the object of the first vision? If you attend to the hieroglyphic, and the exposition which follows; especially when you compare the whole with what is found in the seventh chapter of this book, you will not hesitate to determine, that the great event, which is commonly

called the REFORMATION, was there intended. This happened in the
beginning of the sixteenth century. The first vision, then, respects an
event which we know is accomplished, and has actually happened about
three hundred years ago.

In the third vision the fall of *great Babylon* is predicted. By this
symbolical name is indisputably intended, the seat and dominion of that
powerful adversary, who for many ages has opposed the interests of true
religion, encroached upon the prerogatives of Jesus Christ, and persecuted his faithful followers. The duration of this enemy is limited to
twelve hundred and sixty prophetic years. Different calculations have
been made respecting the time when his reign actually commenced,
which renders it difficult to determine the precise period of his destruction: but the latest date which has been, or, indeed, can be, fixed for
his rise, extends his continuance to the year 1999; consequently his fall
must, at farthest, be immediately before the year 2000, when the Millennium will be fully introduced.

Here, then, we have found two extremes, between which the prediction in question will be fulfilled. It must be after the Reformation,
and before the fall of antichrist. The angel must begin his flight after
the year 1500, and before the year 2000. This brings our inquiry within
the space of five hundred years.

These boundaries will be abridged, when we reflect that three hundred
years have elapsed since the Reformation, and nothing corresponding
to the vision has yet been seen; nothing in respect to the universality,
the power, and success, which characterize the preaching of the Gospel
described in the prediction. Much was confessedly done; great things
were achieved at the Reformation. But this is *another* angel—this fore-
tells *another* preaching, vastly more enlarged and interesting in its
consequences than any thing which happened then, or at any period
since. It delineates an event which, when estimated in all its concurring
circumstances, cannot fail of establishing the conviction, that it is not
yet fulfilled. Three hundred years have passed away, and instead of
increasing, the Church has rather diminished in purity, in zeal, and in
numbers. She has retired, some steps at least, back into the wilderness
again, and doth not now maintain that eminence, nor sing with so el-
evated a note, as when she made her appearance upon Mount Zion at
the Reformation.

We are compelled, therefore, to look forward for the accomplishment;
and are now reduced to the short remaining space of two hundred years.
Within this compass there can be no mistake. At some point of time
from, and including the present day, and before the close of two hundred
years, the angel must begin to fly in the midst of the Churches, and

preach the everlasting Gospel to all nations, and tongues, and kindred, and people in the earth.

Thus far the prophecy, taken in its connection and order, has assisted us in our calculation. We shall, perhaps, approach nearer, if we attend to some momentous EVENTS, which, from the whole tenor of the prophetic word, we know are to happen previous to the Millennium, and consequently, within two hundred years. If these be such as will necessarily require considerable time, and if the event in question be inseparably connected with them, and stand foremost in the series, we may be enabled, from them, to form a rational conclusion of the probable season when this will commence.

The events to which we allude are—the punishment of the nations who aided antichrist in murdering the servants of God—the conversion of the Jews—the bringing in the fulness of the Gentiles—and the fall of mystical Babylon. Whether the order of these events will accord to this enumeration; whether they will begin at once, and move forward together; or whatever may be the length of time between one and the other; our reasoning upon them will not be affected, since they are all to be completed within the space of two hundred years.

It would lead us too far from the subject immediately before us, to discuss the several articles we have stated, to attempt to demonstrate their certainty, or calculate the precise time of their accomplishment; we must here take them for granted, and content ourselves with little more than naming them.

Before we advert, however, to either of these, it may obviate erroneous inferences, and assist in forming a just estimate of the time required for the accomplishment, briefly to premise—that an inviolable harmony for ever subsists between every subordinate event and the great end to which God has always respect in the administration of his providence, and nothing is ever admitted to the injury of this harmony—that the designs of Providence are always executed in a way suited to the subjects to which they relate, and analogous to the usual procedure in similar cases—that, as the attainment of every end is effected by proper means, so the progress which characterizes all the works of God is gradual; and—that we are not permitted to indulge in the marvellous, or expect an unnecessary profusion of miracles, where the end can be obtained by the concurrence of ordinary causes and effects. These are maxims respecting the moral government of God; and in judging of the manner in which those events will be produced, and consequently, in estimating the space of time required for their completion, are to be particularly recollected.

1. We mentioned *the punishment of the nations who aided antichrist*

in murdering the servants of God. That the blood of the martyrs will be avenged, and the wrath of God poured out upon the nations who wickedly shed that blood, is awfully intimated, Rev. vi. 9, 10, 11, and is indisputably confirmed by a solemn appeal to the perfections of Jehovah. Rev. xvi. 5, 6. *Thou art righteous, O Lord, because thou hast judged thus; for they have shed the blood of saints and prophets, and thou hast given them blood to drink; for they are worthy.* The tremendous process of this judgment, whenever it opens, may, by various procedures in Divine Providence, be shortened. The quiver of God is full of arrows. Yet as these nations perpetrated their cruelties by violence, as they slew by the sword, it is probable *they shall perish with the sword.* But, what conflicts; what revolutions; what risings of nations, who are to be the mutual executioners of this terrible sentence, are here implied!

2. *The Jews are to be converted.* That ancient and singular people have long been dispersed throughout the world, without partaking in the government, or mixing in consanguinity with any nation. *For many days*, indeed, they have abode *without a king, and without a prince, without a sacrifice, and without an ephod and teraphim.* Excommunicated by their unbelief, wandering and forlorn, they have long been paying the price of precious blood. Preserved by a particular providence, and perhaps as numerous as ever, they continue monuments of the truth of God in his righteous threatenings, and of the severity of his awful justice. But blessings and honour are in store for that people. They are destined to become equal monuments of the faithfulness of God to his promises, and of the riches of his sovereign grace. The residue of the spirit is with him, and he will *breathe upon these slain, that they may live. God is able to graft them in again,* and has declared he will do it. *All Israel shall be saved.* The Jews will assuredly be converted, and with raptures of faith and love, hail the adorable Jesus as the true Messiah, their Lord and our Lord, their King and our King. To their own land they will also again return, and flourish there, not under the former theocracy, which was blended with rituals now abolished, but under a government adapted to their new and exalted condition. The Lord will rejoice over them to build them up, and do them good, and showers of blessings shall descend upon them. There they will constitute the centre, the most distinguished and dignified point to which the whole Christian Church, throughout the world, will stand related. But to effect all this, admitting the miraculous interposition of divine grace and power, what instruction, what arrangements, what assistance from other nations, what journeyings, what concurring providences, must here combine!

3. *The fulness of the Gentiles* is to be brought into the Church. *If the casting away of the Jews be the reconciling of the world, what shall the receiving of them be, but life from the dead?* Millions have already been gathered from the nations; yet these are only the first fruit, an handful, compared to the harvest *which shall shake like Lebanon.* But what means and ends, what causes and effects, what a train of events are comprized in the conversion of the world to the obedience of Christ! What prejudices must be conquered, what old foundations razed, what new structures erected! The nations must be taught before they can believe or will submit. *How shall they call on him in whom they have not believed? and how shall they believe in him of whom they have not heard? and how shall they hear without a preacher? and how shall they preach except they be sent?* It required forty years to preach the Gospel at first throughout the Roman Empire; and it was three hundred and twenty-five years before the Christian religion publicly triumphed over Pagan idolatry. Should the same Divine Power, the same effusion of the Holy Spirit, even in a more ample measure, be afforded; should Pentecost seasons be frequently repeated, and the *work be cut short,* still a number of years must necessarily elapse in accomplishing this blessed purpose. Scattered over every continent and island between the distant poles; many of the nations uncivilized, depressed in savage ignorance, and degraded in brutal manners; and every carnal mind, in all the nations, at *enmity against God,* and opposed to the Gospel; what materials, what a field, from which to gather so rich a harvest!

4. *The destruction of antichrist,* or the fall of mystical Babylon, was the last thing mentioned. This adversary will certainly be brought down. There shall be nothing left to *hurt nor destroy in all the holy mountain.* Whatever opposes the interests of true religion, in the establishment of any State or Church, will be prostrated. Ecclesiastical dignitaries, spiritual lords, and all the pageantry of the hierarchy, in its various modifications, which have debased the Gospel, and metamorphosed the kingdom of Christ to a kingdom of this world, will be finally trampled in the dust, and despised by Christians. Antichrist is to be consumed *by the Spirit of the mouth of the Lord.* This consumption began at the Reformation, and will increase in the same degree in which the everlasting Gospel is preached with success. But his final destruction will be by judgments, not of correction, but of extermination. Every thing in that system is branded with *perdition.* This is the fatal mark which God has fixed upon antichrist. To the expulsion of whatever offends within the pale of the visible Church, must be annexed the removal of every obstacle which has hitherto prevented the promulgation and prosperity of the Gospel. When the principal enemy, who fixed his seat at

Rome, is destroyed, the eastern antichrist will also be demolished. The powers which support the delusion of Mahomet, with every thing that militates against revealed religion, and the worship of God the Redeemer, throughout the whole earth, shall be overthrown.

What changes in the moral world, what revolutions in the civil, are impending! Attend to each of the enumerated articles; estimate their magnitude; recollect the maxims respecting the procedure of Divine Providence; and then determine, whether two hundred years are not a short space for the consummation of such events? and, if the extensive propagation of the Gospel is to precede the conversion of the Jews, the bringing in of the fulness of the Gentiles, and the destruction of antichrist, say, whether we may not indulge the expectation, that it will soon commence, if it be not already begun? We conclude, without hesitation, that the Churches are authorised to hope that *the vision shall* quickly *speak. It will surely come, it will not tarry.*

With this conclusion, if, now, we compare existing facts; if we view the missionary spirit which has suddenly pervaded the Churches, and estimate the efforts lately made, and still making, for sending the Gospel to those who know not the precious name of Jesus, and are perishing in their sins; do we not discover a striking resemblance of what the vision describes? may we not exclaim, Behold the angel! his flight is begun!

Here our inquiries might rest; yet as this prediction may be comprized also under the *third* class of prophecies, and receives additional light from the rules of explication respecting co-existing events, we must, in justice to the subject, briefly attend to what can be obtained from that source. *The hour of God's judgment*, we have already seen, is mentioned as the very hour when the angel begins to fly. This is a part of his proclamation. Upon this his commission to go forth is expressly sanctioned. To the three other great events which are to happen, the extensive preaching of the Gospel must, in the nature of things, be antecedent, as means to effect those ends; but with the first mentioned it is to be coetaneous. When that begins, this will also commence.

What we are to understand by this *judgment of God* has been explained, and we are assured that, sooner or later —— but we recoil at the exposition, and proceed with reluctance upon a subject which excites such sympathy, such sensibility, so much pain. Yet faithfulness renders it incumbent to say—We are assured that, sooner or later, it will certainly be inflicted upon the nations, in their national capacity, who are chargeable with the murder of the saints. The justice and dignity of the moral government; the veracity of God in fulfilling what he has so repeatedly declared in his word; a vindication of the insulted honour of the Saviour; and his love to his people and cause; all conspire to render this dispensation inevitable. The debt must be paid. The voice of blood will be heard. Believers who reside in those nations, and dread the scene, might as well pray that the Lord would not *be revealed in flaming fire to take vengeance upon them that know not God, and obey not the Gospel of our Lord Jesus Christ;* or, that the elements might be preserved from *melting with fervent heat,* and the world exempted from final conflagration; as to pray that the precious blood of the saints should not be avenged. The righteous may protect the wicked, and, in the ordinary procedures of Providence, avert impending destruction for a time; but although *Noah, Daniel and Job were there,* when this hour of retribution arrives, they could procure no longer forbearance. Conformably to this, his people are not exhorted to pray against the approaching calamity, but to submit in faith and hope; and when the awful season shall arrive, to fly to their chambers and hide themselves. They shall be safely protected. The Lord knoweth how to deliver his children; and will, as when Jerusalem was destroyed, provide some *Pella* for them. *When he maketh inquisition for blood, he remembereth them: he forgetteth not the cry of the humble.*

But when will God perform this strange work? Ah, perhaps it is already begun! What are the singular, what the desolating scenes which have opened, and are still enlarging in prospect? Why are convulsed nations rising in a new and terrific form to exterminate each other? Are these the *beginnings of sorrows?* Are these the first movements for avenging the Saviour's cause? Is God now coming out of his place to judge *the earth,* to judge that portion of the world which assisted the beast in slaying the witnesses? Must the blood, so long covered and forgotten by men, now come in remembrance, and be disclosed! Must this generation —— we forbear. Judge ye. But, be assured, that if this work be begun, or whenever it doth begin, at that very hour the angel will begin to fly. When Zion sings of judgment, she always sings of mercy.

Let this suffice. You have attended to the prophecy, and estimated the period of its accomplishment. You have compared existing facts with the prediction, and drawn a conclusion. Do you now call, *Watchman, what of the night? Watchman, what of the night? The watchman saith, the morning cometh, and also the night.* Clouds and darkness still remain, and the gloom may even thicken at its close; but the rising dawn will soon dispel the shades, and shine *more and more unto the perfect day.* THE MORNING COMETH!

FROM the numerous reflections suggested by this subject, the limits of our discourse permit us to select only a few.

1. HOW MYSTERIOUS are the ways of God! *His way is in the sea, his path in the great waters, and his footsteps are not known.* The time which elapsed before the birth of the Messiah; the narrow boundaries within which the Church was circumscribed during the dispensation of the Old Testament; the sufferings which overwhelmed her immediately after the primitive ages of Christianity; and the small progress of truth and righteousness for so many centuries to the present day, are all, to us, mysterious and inexplicable. What difficulties hold us in suspense! How many inquiries rise! If the everlasting Gospel is to be preached to the whole world, why are the nations permitted to remain so long in ignorance and wickedness? If the heathen be given to the Lord Jesus, why doth he delay to take possession of them? why a discrimination? why —— *But, O man, who art thou that repliest against God? Shall the thing formed say to him that formed it, Why hast thou made me thus?* Can any say unto him, *What dost thou?* Say rather, *O the depth of the riches both of the wisdom and knowledge of God; how unsearchable are his judgments, and his ways past finding out! Even so, Father, for so it seemed good in thy sight!*

Delays have tried the faith and patience of the saints; and scoffers, seizing the occasion, have dared to demand, *Where is the promise of his coming?* But darkness will be succeeded by light, perplexing difficulties all be solved, and apparent confusion terminate in perfect order. Zion shall, before long, cease to complain, that *her Lord hath forgotten her;* and as for the wicked, they may suppress their blasphemies. *The Lord is not slack concerning his promise. Behold the day cometh, too soon for them, the day cometh that shall burn as an oven; and all the proud, yea, and all that do wickedly, shall be stubble.* God will vindicate his ways, and display the harmony which has for ever subsisted between his providence and promises. The period is approaching that will abundantly compensate for the severest trials and the longest delays, a period when the Redeemer's kingdom on earth will perfectly correspond to the sublimest descriptions of its extent and glory. *The Lord reigneth, let the earth rejoice. He will make crooked things straight, and darkness light. As for God, his way is perfect.*

2. The MAGNITUDE of this event next arrests our attention. Vast in its nature and consequences, it involves renovations in the moral world more extensive and stupendous than any hitherto experienced; it implicates radical changes in the manners and customs of mankind; and even comprehends revolutions in the principles and administration of civil government, which surpass the power of anticipation. But vast and difficult as these may appear, there is nothing in their rise, their progress, or their consummation, that implies a contradiction. In the physical

order of things the event is possible; agreeably to the moral system it can be effected; and it certainly is most desirable and devoutly to be wished. When all nations receive the Gospel, and become real Christians; when men of every rank, *from the least to the greatest, shall know the Lord*, and devote themselves to the service of their Redeemer, then all will be happy. Individuals will be happy, society will be happy, and peace, joy, and holiness prevail throughout the whole earth. This is the manifestation for which the world is waiting. The creation, groaning under the complicated miseries introduced by sin, will then obtain the deliverance for which it has been so long in travail.

Alarmed at the prospect, infidels raise formidable objections, and, with infernal malignity, ridicule the hope of believers. *All things*, say they, *all things continue as they were from the beginning of the creation;* and all things will for ever so remain. Nothing can produce the mighty change you Christians contemplate. You cherish fictions, chimeras, and dreams. You draw Elysian scenes which will never be realized. What! convince the ferocious followers of Mahomet that their prophet was an impostor, their Alcoran a rhapsody! persuade the Chinese to abandon their ancient habits! induce the myriads in India to demolish their pagodas, and erect temples to Jesus Christ! curb the roving Tartars! elevate the grovelling Africans! or tame the savages of America! How can these things be? Not by human *might or power*, we reply. We know, more than infidels can inform us, of the stupendous heights and horrid abysses over which the promise has to pass; but none of these things move us. Were it to be accomplished by man; were the subtle counsels of the wise, or the nerved arm of the hero required; the afflicting consequences, in their fullest latitude, would readily be admitted. But it is the work of God. This answers all questions—this silences every cavil. Is any thing too hard for him *that sitteth upon the circle of the earth, and the inhabitants thereof are as grasshoppers?* Are not all things possible with him who *doth according to his will in the army of heaven and among the inhabitants of the earth, and none can stay his hand?* Has the glorified Mediator all power given to him in heaven and in earth to accomplish this very event, and can the faith of his people be chimerical? Are their hopes to be ridiculed? Great as it may be, it is not too great for him to perform. *Every valley shall be exalted, and every mountain and hill shall be made low; and the crooked shall be made straight; and the rough places plain: and the glory of the Lord shall be revealed, and all flesh shall see it together: for the mouth of the Lord hath spoken it.*

3. The CERTAINTY of the accomplishment affords a consoling reflection. This is implied in what has already been said; but it deserves a

more distinct consideration. Christians are not chargeable with enthusiasm when they believe the promises of God will be fulfilled. They
follow no cunningly devised fables when they *make known the power
and coming of the Lord Jesus Christ.* They *speak the words of truth
and soberness,* when they say, the everlasting Gospel will be successfully preached *to all them that dwell on this earth, and to every nation,
and kindred, and tongue, and people.* Always ready to *give a reason of
the hope that is in them,* in regard to their own salvation, they are
equally prepared to vindicate their expectation respecting the enlargement of their Redeemer's kingdom in the world.

The truth of God is pledged to accomplish his word. Nothing can
possibly intervene to change his plan. Nothing can arise to frustrate his
purpose. The Lord has faithfully executed all he promised, in the proper
season, from the beginning of the world; and will he not perfect what
yet remaineth? After preserving his Church under the wasting persecutions of imperial Rome, and the execrable fury of Rome papal; after
hiding her in the wilderness, and nourishing her so long in her adversity;
will he not bring her forth to public view in the beauties of holiness,
*fair as the moon, clear as the sun, and terrible as an army with banners?
As I live, saith the Lord, thou shalt surely clothe thee with them all as
with an ornament, and bind them on thee as a bride doth: I will contend
with him that contendeth with thee, and I will save thy children: all
flesh shall know that I the Lord am thy Saviour and thy Redeemer, the
mighty one of Jacob.*

It is right and proper that Jesus Christ should reign over the whole
world, and that *all nations should serve him.* Is he not worthy, *the
Sceptre of whose kingdom is a Sceptre of righteousness,* to be the *King
of Kings and Lord of Lords?* Is he constituted *the heir of the world,*
and shall he not, in due season, possess his inheritance? Hath he shed
his precious blood upon this earth, and is it not reasonable and fit that
the theatre of his deep humiliation should become also the threatre of
his exalted authority, power and grace? Has the heel of the Saviour
been bruised to the utmost extent of the sentence, and will not the
head of the serpent be broken in the fullest import of the promise? Are
the children of God instructed to plead, that his kingdom may come;
and will not their heavenly Father answer the incessant prayers, which,
for many ages, have addressed his throne? *Shall not God avenge his
own elect which cry day and night unto him, though he bear long with
them? I tell you, that he will avenge them speedily. The kingdom and
dominion, and the greatness of the kingdom under the whole heaven,
shall be given to the people of the saints of the Most High, whose
kingdom is an everlasting kingdom, and all dominions shall serve and*

obey him. The kingdom shall not be left to other people, but it shall break in pieces and consume all these kingdoms, and it shall stand for ever. Remove the diadem and take off the crown. I will overturn, overturn, overturn it, and it shall be no more, until he come WHOSE RIGHT IT IS; *and I will give it him.*

Before the Messiah came, his people were wearied with waiting. Many conjectures and errors prevailed among the Jews in their calculations and expectations. But seasons, and years, and ages revolved; and changes and revolutions in the nations and kingdoms of the earth succeeded; until the *fulness of time* arrived, and then the Saviour was born. So among Christians, there may be misapprehensions concerning the nature and extent of the blessings promised to the Church; erroneous conclusions may be formed respecting the time when the happy period we contemplate will commence; but, *in the end, the vision shall speak.* Seasons, and years, and ages will revolve; and changes and revolutions in the nations and kingdoms of the earth succeed, until the day *dawns and the day-star arises,* and then *the dominion, and glory, and kingdom, shall be given to him, that all people, nations and languages shall serve him.* Nothing on the part of sinners prevented his coming in the flesh; and all the ignorance of mankind, the prejudice of unbelief, the malice of infidelity, and the combined powers of earth and hell, will not delay his coming, with his Gospel and Spirit, agreeably to his promise. *God is not a man, that he should lie, neither the son of man, that he should repent: hath he said, and shall he not do it? or hath he spoken, and shall he not make it good? I the Lord will hasten it in his time.*

Come, *let us walk about Zion and go round about her,* let us *tell the towers thereof and mark well her bulwarks.* The Church, from the beginning, had been greatly circumscribed, and was still a small flock when our Lord was upon earth. It has continued comparatively small for many centuries, and few have even hitherto entered in at the straight gate, contrasted with the multitude who choose the broad way *that leadeth to destruction.* But *glorious things are spoken of the city of God.* The interests of religion shall not always be thus depressed. The Church of Christ will emerge from obscurity, and the number of his followers not be small. Nothing is more certain, than that God has promised a great enlargement of the kingdom of the Redeemer in this world, with abundant communications of his spirit and presence. In the most unequivocal language it is foretold, that all people and nations throughout the whole earth shall be instructed in the true religion, and brought into the Church of God. *All dominions shall serve and obey him. All nations shall serve him. All nations shall call him blessed. In him shall all the nations of the earth be blessed. He will destroy the covering cast over all people, and the veil that is spread over all nations. All flesh shall see the salvation of the Lord. Unto him shall all flesh come. The earth shall be full of the knowledge of the Lord, as the waters cover the seas.* In this the promises of the Old as well as of the New Testament completely harmonize. They all establish the desirable fact, that a period will most assuredly arrive, when there shall not be one nation in the world which shall not embrace the Christian religion. *The nation and kingdom which shall not serve thee shall perish, yea, these nations shall be utterly wasted.*

A time will therefore come when the knowledge of the truth shall universally prevail, and holiness shall characterize the world: a time when the Church shall be known and acknowledged to be but one, a dignified and excellent society, connected in the most perfect order, and shining in the light of the Sun of Righteousness: a time when the world shall be delivered from the evils and calamities under which it has so long groaned, and the blessing of God the Redeemer be upon all the families of the earth. *Then the wilderness and the solitary place shall be glad, and the desert shall rejoice and blossom as the rose.* Then *let the wilderness and the cities lift up their voices; let the villages, the inhabitants of the rock, sing; let them shout from the top of the mountains, let them give glory unto the Lord, and declare his praise in the islands.*

These promises have not yet been fulfilled. There has never been any propagation of true religion that corresponds to the universality indicated in the promises. Where the word and ordinances have been hitherto known and enjoyed, their blessed influence upon the hearts and conduct of men has not been thus powerfully experienced. And countless millions, throughout the earth, have never heard that there is a Saviour.

To the fulfilment of these promises, it is necessary that the Gospel be sent to every nation in the world. The preached word is the established mean for converting sinners, and without the mean the end will not be obtained. *The preaching of the cross* is unto them which are saved *the power of God.* It hath pleased him, *by the foolishness of preaching, to save them that believe.* If, therefore, the blessings promised are to be conferred, there will also come a time when God will send his everlasting Gospel to every people, tongue, and kindred in the earth. This time, we believe, is arrived. The present exertions in the Churches, we are persuaded, are the first stirrings, the gradual beginnings for accomplishing that great end.

Eventful period! a time replete with occurrences of the highest importance to the world! Long lives for many generations have passed in uniform succession, and men have grown old without witnessing any remarkable deviation from the ordinary course of Providence. But now a new era is commencing. The close of the last, and the opening of the present century, exhibit strange and astonishing things. Principles and achievements, revolutions and designs, events uncommon and portentous, in rapid succession, arrest our attention. Each year, each day, is pregnant with something great, and all human calculations are set at defiance. The infidel, with his impious philosophy, stands aghast, and, destitute of resources, with trembling forebodings, wonders how and where the perplexed scene will end; whilst the Christian, instructed by the word and spirit of his Saviour, calmly views the turning of the dreadful wheels, and knows which way they proceed. Strengthened by divine grace, he stands undaunted in the mighty commotion, and looks up, rejoicing that his prayers are heard, and that his *redemption draweth nigh.*

4. How influential the MOTIVE suggested by this prediction to engage in strenuous exertions to propagate the Gospel! how forcible the argument to persevere in the benevolent work! When *Daniel understood by books the number of years, whereof the word of the Lord came to Jeremiah the prophet,* his attention was fixed; his affections were raised; and it operated as a motive to intercede for the accomplishment of the prophecy; agreeably to the maxim, that God *will be inquired of by the house of Israel to do it for them.* The pious captives, anxiously waiting for their restoration, were, no doubt, instructed by *Daniel,* and joined with him in supplicating the throne of grace. The word passed rapidly among the scattered families, and they gladly prepared for the impending change. It is supposed that *Daniel,* who, from his former station at the king's court, might easily obtain access to *Cyrus,* communicated to that prince, with suitable and successful arguments, the part assigned in prophecy for him to fulfil. In this way the prophet was instrumental in Divine Providence to bring forward the completion of the promise. He united exertions with his prayers. He felt the influence of the motive: and *the grace which was bestowed upon him was not in vain.*

In like manner, let Christians now be wise, and receive instruction. *Ye, Brethren, are not in darkness that that day should overtake you as a thief. Ye are all the children of light, and the children of the day; we are not of the night nor of darkness, therefore let us not sleep as do others, but let us watch and be sober.* It is time for the wise virgins who have slumbered *to arise and trim their lamps.* The cry is made, BEHOLD THE BRIDEGROOM COMETH! he cometh to send his Gospel abroad, and bless the world with his truth and righteousness.

It is an honour to be employed in the service of the Redeemer. *I had rather be a door-keeper in the house of my God, than to dwell in the tents of wickedness.* It is a privilege to be *labourers together with God.* It is a pleasant work, to *go up to the mountain and bring wood and build the house,* when we are convinced the time is come, and the Lord saith, *he will take pleasure in it, and will be glorified.*

Every motive which stimulates to vigorous efforts in propagating the Gospel, derives additional force and energy from this word of prophecy. Is the glory of God an impressive argument? Attend to the prediction before us, and be encouraged to hope, that God, who hath glorified his holy name, will soon *glorify it again.* He will make himself known throughout the whole earth, not only in his divine perfections, as the one only true God, but in the adorable manner of his existence, as Father, Son, and Holy Ghost; and will be worshipped every where in the blessed relation of REDEEMER as well as Creator.—Doth the love of Christ constrain? Have you crowned him with your homage, and often grieved at the contempt cast upon his precious name and cause? See what is doing in the Churches! To him every knee will bow; *the Most Mighty is girding his sword upon his thigh; the arm of the Lord will awake as in the ancient days, in the generations of old; and the people shall fall under him. His name shall endure for ever.*—Are you affected with the deplorable condition of the greatest part of the world, which lieth in ignorance and wickedness? Behold the everlasting Gospel is going forth to every tongue, and kindred, and nation, and shall universally prevail. Yet a little while, and *the people that walk in darkness will see a great light, and upon them that dwell in the land of the shadow of death will the light shine.*—All the precepts which are our warrant to engage in this work; all the promises which are our encouragement to persevere with firmness, receive new weight and influence. While we are musing upon the prediction before us, *our hearts are hot within us; the fire burns;* zeal kindles to a flame; we glow with ardour to perform our part, and assist the flight of the preaching angel. We live to see the dawn; we long to see the day. We witness at least the beginnings of what *many prophets and righteous men have desired to see, and have not seen them.* For those of us who are advanced in years, let this suffice. We now can depart in peace. We shall hear of the accomplishment, and join with those who rejoice in heaven, over sinners who are converted. But you, my younger Brethren, indulge the pleasant view, and enter with vigour into the labours before you. *Lift up your eyes, and look on the fields, for they are white already to harvest.* Go on and prosper in your work. Derive wisdom, strength, and grace from your exalted Jesus. *Be of good courage, and behave valiantly. Watch*

*ye, stand fast in the faith, quit ye like men, be strong. The Lord will go
before you, and the God of Israel will be your reward.*

5. Let MISSIONARY SOCIETIES ascend the prophetic mount, and enjoy
the vast prospect laid open to their view. Let them appreciate as they
ought, the eminent station assigned them by their Saviour, and obtain
grace to be found faithful. They are employed by him, in the midst of
the Churches, to accomplish his blessed purposes, and fulfil his word.
By their agency the preaching angel commences his flight, and through
their instrumentality the treasure of the Gospel will be brought to all
the nations of the earth. By such associations and efforts it might be
expected the scene would open. *Not by might nor by power*, not from
carnal policy, or by the combination and support of civil rulers, but *by
the Spirit of the Lord*, exciting his ministers and people, from the purest
principles, to execute *the mystery of his will*. The hearts of all men are
in his hand. He can gird and counsel those whom he honours with his
service, to perform any thing he pleaseth. Missionary societies are,
therefore, to be considered as ministering servants, employed in a work
well pleasing to God; and deserving, while they faithfully persevere,
the esteem and affection of all good men.

Be not discouraged, my Brethren, when you inquire, Whom shall we
send, and *who will go for us?* The Lord can provide instruments for his
own work. *Pray ye, therefore, the Lord of the harvest, that he will
send forth labourers into his harvest.* He will hear your prayers, and
raise up missionaries. But with your prayers unite the means for obtaining suitable characters. Reflect seriously whether it would not be
advisable to institute a THEOLOGICAL SCHOOL, for the express purpose
of instructing and preparing pious young men for this arduous service—
whether such an institution would not probably stimulate some to offer
themselves; and certainly produce the highest assurance, that the angels
who go out from the midst of the Churches are well established in the
truth, and will carry the everlasting Gospel in its *purity* abroad. If this
be acceptable to the Lord, he will incline the hearts of his people to
assist you. *The earth* also shall *help the woman*. To accomplish this
measure, the respective societies in America might correspond upon
the subject, and, after due consultation, mutually adopt such plans as
might be judged the most practicable and best calculated to answer the
important object in view. *To him that knoweth to do good, and doeth
it not, to him it is sin.—The King's business requireth haste.*

We, my Brethren, were not the first who engaged in this benevolent
design; but we stand foremost in our opportunities for usefulness and
access to the heathen. Our Brethren in Europe have achieved great
things. Involved in complicated troubles, and the field of their labours

at an immense distance from them, they have, notwithstanding, formed noble designs, and executed them with astonishing promptitude and success. Our situation is happily the reverse. We enjoy tranquillity and rest. There is not a nation at present on earth permitted to threaten or disturb our repose. Our borders are extensively enlarged; and the heathen to whom the Gospel, in the first instance, is to be sent, are near at hand. Already we have found a door of entrance opened, and the neighbouring tribes are becoming friendly to missions: they stretch out the imploring hand; they cry with affecting importunity, *Come over and help us!* This is not merely the language of their real necessity; it has been expressed by their chiefs, with an earnestness and solemnity which evinced their esteem for the Gospel. Should success not always attend your efforts, be not, my Brethren, discouraged. Wait patiently for the precious fruit. The apostles themselves were not always prosperous in every place; nor did the seed sown immediately spring up. Only be faithful; look to your divine Master for direction, depend upon his grace, and leave the issue to him. Be assured your labour shall not be in vain. *Believe in the Lord your God, so shall ye be established; believe his prophets, so shall ye prosper.*

But recollect the work in which we are engaged involves great and unavoidable expenses. The maintaining of missionaries; the erecting and supporting schools among the savages; and many necessary contingent charges, amount to a considerable sum. Without any fund prepared for these purposes, we depend chiefly upon the contribution of members, and the collections made at our monthly and anniversary meetings. It is incumbent, therefore, upon me, to remind you of this before we close. To attain the end we must attend to the means.

Every motive which urges to propagate the Gospel is an argument to excite to extensive liberality. The heathen, in whose behalf I solicit your benevolence, are poor; in every sense of the word, they are poor indeed. In what way can charity be better bestowed? To what higher purpose can you employ your property? What object so affecting to a sympathising heart? What design so interesting to an informed and pious mind? It is a branch of that love which is due to your neighbour; it is an expression of that homage you owe your Redeemer. To him, if you have experienced the power of divine grace, you have devoted your persons and all you possess. *The silver is his, and the gold is his.* To promote his gracious designs of restoring peace, holiness, and happiness to a miserable world, *let all that be round about him bring presents unto him that ought to be feared.*

When Christians of every denomination shall obtain more information upon the subject of missions, and rightly estimate the importance of the work, they will consider it a duty and privilege to become members of societies formed upon principles so disinterested and excellent. Where such societies exist, they will gladly join them; and in districts where none have yet been established, they will heartily unite to form similar institutions. None were ever injured by serving the divine Redeemer. The Churches which exert themselves to send his Gospel to the perishing heathen, may hope to *see his power and glory in the sanctuary*, as the gracious fruit of their prayers and labours.

When Christians learn to compare the providence of God with the word of his prophecy, and see the completion of the promises approaching, they will gladly *open their treasures*, and *present their gifts unto* Jesus. When they believe that his voice, *which shook the earth*, will *once more shake not the earth only, but also the heaven;* that the world and the Church may be prepared, in its fullest extent, to *receive a kingdom which cannot be moved;* they will *not refuse* nor *turn away from him that speaketh from heaven:* they will esteem Zion their chief joy, *and favour the dust thereof.*—HE THAT HATH AN EAR, LET HIM HEAR WHAT THE SPIRIT SAITH UNTO THE CHURCHES.

And now, my Brethren, *despise not the day of small things;* complain not that *you have laboured in vain, and spent your strength for nought:* for yet a little while, and you or your children shall see, and hear of *greater things than these.* The Lord will *show thee great and mighty things which thou knowest not.* The voice of the trumpet will sound *long,* and *wax louder and louder.* You will hear of judgments which shall make the ears to *tingle;* and of mercies you will also hear; for, *from the uttermost parts of the earth we shall hear songs, even glory to the righteous.*

The Church of Christ, we trust, hath survived her worst days; or if conflicts sharp and severe should still be in reserve, we may assuredly consider the present efforts to propagate the Gospel as a precious token for good. It is an earnest of the revival of religion at home, and a pledge of salvation to perishing heathen abroad. Who that sympathises with the miseries of the human family, can fail to rejoice in observing the people of the Lord, of different denominations, uniting their counsels and exertions in this benevolent work! Who that can estimate the necessity and excellence of the doctrines of grace, will not view with raptures of gratitude and praise, an approaching period, when the ignorant will be instructed, the vicious reclaimed, and the religion of the blessed Jesus universally prevail! Without indulging in expectations too sanguine, or anticipating a rapid and uninterrupted series of successes, in which no delays or discouragements will interpose, we wait in confidence for the full accomplishment of the promise, and participate gladly in THE TRIUMPH OF THE GOSPEL.

What John in vision saw, we now behold an existing fact. We see *another angel flying in the midst of heaven, having the everlasting Gospel to preach unto them that dwell on the earth.* With fervent prayers and raised affections we cordially *bid him God speed.* Go, welcome messenger of good tidings, bear the invaluable treasure *to every nation, and kindred, and tongue, and people.* Proclaim *with a loud voice,* that *the hour of his judgment is come;* cry aloud, spare not, until the whole world shall learn to *fear God, to give glory to him,* and *worship him* as their CREATOR AND REDEEMER. *Amen.*

II

James Spencer Cannon, 1776-1852

A student of Livingston and of Livingston's colleague, Solomon Froeligh, Dr. Cannon served New Brunswick as instructor and professor of
ecclesiastical history, church government, and pastoral theology for the
last twenty-six years of his life. The following excerpts from his *Lectures
on Pastoral Theology*, published after his death, show the influence of
Livingston's type of missionary theology, and the revivalistic spirit and
methods so important in the first half of the nineteenth century.

From *Lectures on Pastoral Theology*

OFFERING UP PRAYER IN SOCIAL WORSHIP

Of pastoral prayer, as it is a *gift*, I have spoken in Lectures IV. and V.; but pastoral prayer, as well as preaching, sustains another character. It is *an important duty* of the sacred ministry; and in this light I shall now consider it.

The apostles, in actual service after the day of Pentecost, were bound by their office "to give themselves to *prayer*," as well as to "the ministry of the Word." These words express clearly the fact, that while pastors are to pray in their closets and in their families, like all other Christians who walk along the heavenly road, and "follow on to know the Lord," they are to be engaged in prayer, while leading in *the worship of Christian assemblies*, as their frequent and set business, and to be employed in the same duty, *in visiting families* under their care, especially when they attend on the sick, the afflicted, and troubled in mind.

For the performance of this duty, as well as that of preaching the Word, the pastor, as I have before said, should "covet the best gifts," and seek to do his work with a praying heart, and in an edifying manner. The preparations, on his part, for this particular service, have been adverted to in the fifth Lecture. It remains here to remind you, that it will be highly advantageous to the young pastor, to store his memory with those passages of Scripture which are petitions to God by the pious of former times, and which may be easily converted into supplication now: for religion in every age is the same in its nature, and "the just," from Abel down, have lived by faith and prayed "in the Holy Ghost;" also to write down and commit to memory those petitions which constitute the substance of prayer, and apply to the circumstances of particular Christian congregations, and to the state of the Church at large; and especially, in public pastoral prayer, to remember that believers in Christ are "all members of one body," and that it is the duty of ministers to recognize this fact, and to pray, not only for a particular church, but,

1. For "*all the saints that are in the earth.*" Ephes. vi. 18: "Praying always with all prayer and supplication in the Spirit, and watching thereunto with all perseverance and supplication *for all saints.*"

Is it asked why pastors should pray in a particular manner, and with

28

great engagedness of spirit, for all the saints? I reply, that this duty results—

(1). From *the near relation* which Christians sustain to one another; a relation more intimate, honorable, and lasting, than that which children sustain to their parents.

Children and other earthly kindred are bound to us by blood and natural affection; but death soon severs this feeble tie. Saints are united by one Holy Spirit together in one Lord. The chord which connects them is a heavenly and everlasting one, and their transition from this life to a future one will serve to bind them still closer. In heaven, shall be fully exhibited that glorious union of the saints to one another, and of all to himself, for which the Saviour prayed and died: "I in them, and thou in me, that they may be one, even as we are one; that they may be made perfect in one." (John xvii. 22, 23.)

But the union of believers to Christ *is most intimate*. There is a mysterious glory in it. The connecting tie is that Holy Spirit whose work is perfect; and in heaven, where "the Lamb's wife," having made herself ready, shall appear "without spot or wrinkle," that union shall be manifested in all its extent and perfection. But let me hasten to say, that, standing here thus united to Christ and to "all the saints," our prayers must correspond with that high relation. As being "partakers of the same divine nature," as children by regeneration and adoption of one heavenly Father, as members of the same body, as soldiers engaged under one chief in the same conflict, as travellers on the same highway, and as fellow-heirs of an eternal inheritance in glory, the saints should occupy a particular place in our supplications. With what weight did their spiritual prosperity press upon the hearts of the apostles! "I have," said John, "no greater joy than that my children walk in the truth." "I live," said Paul, "if ye stand fast in the Lord." So now we must habitually say at the throne of grace, "Let there be dew upon Israel;" "Feed thine inheritance, and lift them up for ever;" "Help, Lord! for the godly man ceaseth;" "Let grace abound to all who love our Lord Jesus Christ in sincerity;" "For my brethren and companions' sake, we must say, Peace be within thee: because of the house of the Lord our God, I will seek thy good."

(2.) The duty of praying for "all saints" also results from the fact, that they are *"the excellent of the earth"*—"a chosen generation"—"a holy nation." Their moral worth is vastly greater than that of multitudes of ungodly men, formed into either civil or literary societies. They constitute "the house of the Lord"—"the habitation of God, through the Holy Spirit"—"a building fitly framed together, and growing up into an holy temple in the Lord"—"a body, joined together, and compacted by that which every joint supplieth, and in which there is to be an effectual working, in the measure of every part, to the increase of the whole." (Ephes. ii. 21; iv. 16.)

But will not God surely bring his saints to the enjoyment of ever-lasting glory? and if he will preserve them unto his heavenly kingdom, do they not stand in less need of our prayers than those who are still afar off? Jehovah, it is true, who hath effectually called, will glorify his saints. But, be it observed, that there is an established order in accomplishing this work, and *that order* requires the intervention of the prayers of the Church. If, therefore, we desire that our fellow-travellers on the heavenly road shall be supported and guided all their journey through, we must pray especially for them. "I, the Lord, have spoken it, and I will do it." Is it then unnecessary to pray? No, indeed; for it is immediately added, "Thus saith the Lord, Yet for all these things I will be inquired of by the house of Israel, to do it for them."

In praying for all the saints, the pastor will remember, of course, that portion of them which is committed to his pastoral care, and will supplicate with a special reference to the states of those of this number who are involved in trouble of mind, laboring under the pressure of affliction, exposed to any threatening evil, or giving any evidence of backsliding, though such may not be present in the worshipping assembly.

Prayer for those who decline in religion is always better received than reproof, and may be happily used for their recovery when reproof would be an imprudent measure. But let no pastor discover his displeasure at particular persons by his public prayers. Those who do this, degrade the sacred office: "they know not what manner of spirit they are of." Compassion and benevolence towards others must leaven our hearts in prayer; otherwise we cannot say, as our Lord hath taught us, "Forgive us our trespasses, as we forgive those who trespass against us."

There may be occasions on which a minister of the Word is unjustly treated by persons under his pastoral care, and it may be his duty to complain of such at the throne of grace. In those cases, let his complaints be made in secret prayer, and his supplications be offered up at the same time for the conversion of all who despitefully use him and persecute him.

2. Another prominent subject of petition in public prayer by the pastor is, *the conversion of sinners.* For this end the ministry was instituted; for this end the gospel is to be preached. The conversion of sinners is necessary to the perpetuation of the Church: hence our Lord directed his disciples to pray, "thy kingdom come," and to be solicitous that more laborers should be sent into the harvest-field. Especially

should pastors pray that sinners should be turned from their evil ways to God: for this is the Divine command, "Ye that make mention of the Lord, keep not silence, and give him no rest until he make Jerusalem a name and a praise in the earth."

Supplication of this kind, is but asking a blessing upon a pastor's own labors in the field. How then can he forbear to entreat that the Word may be accompanied with Divine power, and that new accessions may be made to the sacramental host of God? This part of duty in prayer is scarcely ever neglected.

It has however been asked, How far is a pastor authorized to pray for any particular person by name, who is in a distant land and remote from the worshipping assembly? For instance: A minister in one of our city churches prayed that God would bless a convert from Islamism in Asia, mentioning him by name, "if he were yet alive." Is such an act to be commended and imitated? In reply to these questions, I would observe, first, that mentioning names in public prayer, even of those who belong to the society, after their names have been read, with their request for the prayer of the church, is not necessary, and by no means to be commended; second, that it is hardly to be permitted that a pastor shall introduce by name, in public prayer, a person who is a stranger to the greater part of the church, and of whose particular circumstances, from his remote situation, we can have no knowledge at the present time. Prayer is an act of *social* worship. The church must pray with the understanding, as well as with the heart. Every duty of the church in relation to the welfare of her distant members, will be comprehended in her supplications for "all the saints."

3. A third prominent subject of petition by the pastor in public social worship, is, *the enlargement of the visible Church of God in this world*. This, you will perceive, is connected with the duty of praying for the conversion of sinners, through the effectual operation of the Word just preached upon the hearts of those who heard it. This latter has more particularly in view the conversion of those who enjoy, in Christian lands, the ministrations of the gospel: but the former has respect to missionary efforts; to the conversion of nations still in darkness; to the spread of truth abroad; and to the removal of all those obstacles which have hitherto obstructed the onward march of pure Christianity, and checked the enlargement of the Church among the Gentiles.

Early in the dispensation of mercy to the human family, did God declare, that through the appointed Redeemer, "the seed of Abraham," all the families of the earth should be blessed. With delight did the saints subsequently dwell upon this fact, that all nations should see the salvation of God, and that all "should call him blessed who should procure that salvation, and the whole earth in process of time be filled with his glory." The promised Saviour came to Zion; he wrought gloriously, triumphed over the prince of darkness, and made not Jerusalem and Judea only, but the whole world, the theatre of his operations. The Gentiles were called; parts of the earth were enlightened and Christianized; but much land remains to be conquered and possessed by the tribes. And are they not at this day moving, and going up to the noble conflict; and shall not prayer be incessantly made by pastors for their success? Surely, the words of the prophet mark out the duty of every Christian minister in this respect: "For Zion's sake I will not hold my peace, for Jerusalem's sake I will not rest, until the righteousness thereof go forth as brightness, and the salvation thereof as a lamp that burneth." (Isa. lxii. 1.)

For encouragement in thus praying, how much hath God spoken in his Word! How numerous and rich are his promises! What glorious things are spoken of the final victory of Zion over all her foes! "Her King shall reign from sea to sea, from the rivers unto the ends of the earth." "All the Gentiles shall see thy righteousness," saith the prophet Isaiah, "and all kings thy glory."

The last clause of this prophecy, a Jewish writer has used as an argument against the Christian faith. "It is here promised to Zion," he says, "that the Israel of God shall be very glorious in the days of the Messiah, so that all kings shall submit to him, and see the glory of his Church: but this has not yet been fulfilled, therefore the Messiah has not yet come."

I reply, briefly, that this prediction cannot refer to the day of the Messiah's manifestation in the flesh, for the same prophet tells us that then he should "be despised and rejected of men." But the prophecy must refer to events under the new dispensation, to be introduced by the Messiah in person. Now that dispensation actually came after the day of Pentecost. It still exists, but is not yet terminated. Before it closes, the prediction, which is now in progress, shall receive its full and glorious accomplishment. "All the Gentiles shall come to the light of the Church, and all kings shall see her glory."

In looking back on past dispensations, we find that God has exercised a sovereign pleasure with respect to the exact times when he should fulfil his Word. He promised to give to Abraham's descendants by Sarah the whole of the land of Canaan. This promise was partially fulfilled in the days of Joshua, but its complete fulfilment did not occur until the reigns of David and Solomon. So it will be at the "end of these days," that the predictions and promises in relation to the glory of the Church shall receive their full accomplishment.

Besides, it is to be remembered that the predicted glory of the Church shall consist in her purity and spirituality, and not in worldly grandeur and visible splendor.

Here, while pressing the duty of pastoral prayer for the enlargement of the Church throughout the earth, let me remind you that it was usual with the primitive Christians to pray for the conversion of the whole world to the gospel faith. This fact, which is very interesting to us, we are told by Father Origen, that "The Gentiles wondered, when they heard such prayer drop from the lips of the despised Nazarenes, who were but as a handful of corn upon the top of the mountains." Celsus, the philosopher, whose heart was fired with rage against the Christians, raised a contemptuous laugh at what he considered to be an absurd and extravagant prayer. He said: "ὅτι ὁ τουτο οιομενος, οιδεν ουδεν;" that is, "he thought such a universal agreement in one mode of religious belief a perfect chimera, and those who prayed for it deserved the contempt of men of understanding."

Regardless of the sneers of this self-conceited philosopher, the Christians continued to pray for the conversion of the world, until corruptions seated themselves in the vitals of the Church, and many lights in her courts were extinguished. Some thought that the external prosperity of the Church under the reign of Constantine, was the promised millennium! The Scriptures on this subject were sadly misinterpreted. Presently, as the darkness thickened under the sway of "the man of sin, seated in the temple of God," the principal doctrines of the gospel were untaught; the prophecies relating to the subjection of the whole world to the Saviour's sceptre, were not studied in their series and connection; and, down to A.D. 1600, the ancient prayer for the "conversion of the world," excepting as this event was contemplated in the Lord's Prayer, was no longer heard in the churches. The book of Revelation by John, beyond the first three chapters, was a sealed book.

But it pleased God, as years rolled away, after the Reformation, to awaken the minds of certain learned and pious men to the study of the prophecies of Daniel and Isaiah, in connection with those things which the apostle John on the isle of Patmos heard and saw in vision. The result was, the fullest conviction that the conversion of the whole world was promised and predicted. God has so spoken; his words admitted of no other interpretation; the nations should be blessed with the blessing of faithful Abraham; the whole earth should be filled with the knowledge and glory of the Saviour. Another result was, the revival in the churches of the prayer of the primitve Christians for "the conversion of the world." The Church of Scotland by her "Memorial," stirred up the hearts of Christians to pray every where for the enlargement of the Church by missionary efforts, for the liberation of all nations from the power of the prince of darkness, and from the fetters of gross error, superstition, and wickedness.

Let, then, the pastor pray especially for this great mercy. Let him supplicate, that millions yet unborn may see the salvation of God, and that the glory of the Divine Redeemer may be displayed before all people, and his Spirit descend like floods upon the dry ground.

(Special Visitations—The Awakened)

There can be no substitute for actual Christian experience of the power of divine grace.

But, admitting a minister is a converted man, he requires, for this duty, careful study of the operations of sin and grace in his own heart. He should be able to discriminate between the operations of the Holy Spirit and the workings of sin under all its disguises.

(1.) The first thing to be noted by the pastor is, that there are *degrees in awakening.*

i. Every *little concern of mind* is not that awakening from the sleep of sin which results in an anxiety to be interested in the salvation which is by Jesus Christ. Thousands are afraid to die; and the fear of death occasionally produces serious thoughts; and such thoughts will induce one "to walk softly." Now such concern of mind in men is generally eased off by offering up a prayer or two in secret, by reforming a little and doing a few good works; without any perception of the evil of sin, of the enmity of the heart against God, and of the ill-desert of the sinner.

Such concern of mind is not uncommon where Christians live and the gospel is preached; and if ministers, anxious to fill their churches with professors, are satisfied with such awakening, if it be followed by a general profession to believe in Christ, the consequence will be most unhappy in the churches. Professors of religion will abound, who have "a name to live, but are dead." Those professors after a little while will show the unregenerate disposition of their hearts, by disliking the doctrines of grace, by siding with ministers who oppose them, and by crying up a system of doing, doing, doing, as soothing to their own self-righteous propensities.

Carefully, therefore, must the faithful pastor teach, that such slight awakening is no sufficient preparation for either an evangelical repentance, or a cordial reception of Christ as "the Lord our righteousness."

I say, *with the heart:* for not a few, and among them ministers of the gospel too, doctrinally assent to the article of "justification by faith without works," while practically they reject it, and live after all upon their own religious character and doings.

Very carefully must the pastor open the deceits of sin under such slight concern of mind, and inculcate that the *last thing* which the sinner forsakes in coming to Christ is, *reformed and religious self.* The pride of the heart never will submit to the righteousness of God. How very much it looks like a dereliction of self, when a sinner in his agony of mind is heard to say, "that he would be willing to give the whole world, if he had it, to obtain an interest in Christ;" yet, after all, this is only the deceitful working of a self-righteous spirit, that is anxious to give something, and to have *a price in its own hand* for salvation, rather than receive that salvation as it is offered, "without money and without price."

But while the pastor is not to attach great importance to slight concern of mind, he must be equally careful not to treat it *as stark naught;* for there may be in it the commencement of a work of the Holy Spirit in awakening. He must rejoice to see any thoughtless sinner beginning to think seriously; and he must endeavor to render such serious thoughts deeper and more enlightened.

ii. But in the souls of some, the pastor will find a *stronger work* of conviction. They are greatly alarmed at their danger; they perceive their sins to be many and great; they are lost and undone in themselves; they acknowledge that their condemnation is just; they fear they may be damned for ever, and in deep anxiety they pray much, read much, and hasten to hear the Word.

Under this degree of conviction and awakening, the pastor will rejoice to discover the manifest working of the Holy Spirit, "in turning up the fallow ground," before he sows the seeds of divine life.

But he must be careful to teach that such awakening and distress *is not conversion.*

First. He must now, in a particular manner, expose the workings of *self-righteousness,* lest the awakened should rest on a sandy foundation. For, when sinners are thoroughly awakened without being converted, they are strongly excited to acquire such a degree of personal improvement in goodness as may not altogether purchase pardon, but may in a greater or less degree recommend them to the mercy of God in Christ. They expect to gain this by their frequent and fervent prayers, by their reformations, by their care to avoid sin, by enlisting in the ranks of those who try to do good in various ways: and in this very course some persevere and are lost.

Second. Now the pastor must exert himself in exposing the deceitfulness and self-righteousness of the human heart. He must strip the sinner of his remaining rags. He must break him down, by examining into his views and ends in praying and in doing good, and show that these are defective and insufficient.

Third. He must preach Christ in his offices a great deal, and show that there is but one salvation, and that is by grace alone. He must aim to bring the awakened to lie at the mercy-seat, and proclaim that Jesus will surely save such, and such alone. "For he satisfieth the hungry with good things, but sendeth the rich empty away."

iii. But once more; there are instances of awakening power under the gospel Word, that exhibit the distressed mind *sinking into despair!* These call for the special attention of a pastor, and require careful treatment. Such awakened sinners think "there is no mercy for them; that they must be lost for ever; that their damnation is certain," for various reasons. The one so concludes, because he has been uncommonly wicked, and his sins are too great to be pardoned; another, because he has sinned away his choicest opportunities and his former convictions, and it is now too late to seek and hope for pardon; a third, because he has sinned against the Holy Ghost; a fourth, because his seeking has had no happy result; he has grown worse, and heaven is shut against him, and God is more and more hostile to him.

First. In cases of this kind, let the pastor be very serious: for the temptations of the adversary in such desponding minds are unusually strong, and lead sometimes to thoughts of self-destruction, and often to an unwillingness to read the Scriptures, to pray any more, or even to listen to religious conversation; and in a few cases, the temptations of Satan are aided by nervous disorders and a morbid imagination.

Second. In dealing with such distressed persons, let the pastor bring their case in prayer before God in his closet, and ask Christians to do the same; and,

Third. As the despair of the mind in such instances springs from various thoughts, let the pastor reply to each. If it arises from a sense of great sinfulness, let the infinite value of the atonement be dwelt upon; the power of Jesus to save the chief of sinners be preached; the examples in Scripture of such saved, be called up; and the invitations of the Saviour be opened and renewed. Let the distressed read Bunyan and Newton. If despair is created by the sense of opportunities and convictions misimproved, let the pastor proclaim that the door is not shut; that God is still waiting to be gracious; and that the concern of mind on this subject is of itself an evidence that the Spirit of God is not withdrawn, and that salvation is not denied. If the mind is occupied with the belief "that the sin against the Holy Ghost has been committed," let the pastor, in his visits to such, begin with prayer to God for special aid; then speak of the many godly persons who in seasons of darkness and temptation have judged wrong about their state; and of some who thought they had committed the unpardonable sin, and who afterwards saw they were mistaken, and recovered all their peace and comfort; if the pastor can in these cases mention names, with the histories of the persons, it will be better; (and for such purpose, every Christian pastor should be a reader of the lives and experience of godly persons;) and thence let him conclude, that in a matter involving our eternal hopes and God's mercy in Christ, we should not be hasty in our judgment, but take time and reflect long, with earnest prayer. And,

Finally. Let the pastor afterwards proceed to speak of the nature of the sin against the Holy Ghost, inquiring whether it is a sin which can be committed at this day. For some think that it was a sin peculiar to the apostolic day, or the age of miracles; for as it formed an extraordinary case under the dispensations of grace, it seemed to require a sinning against the extraordinary light which miracles afforded of the truth of Christianity.

But if the pastor thinks that the sin *can now be committed*, let him open its nature by showing that it is made up of *knowledge* and *enmity* against Christ and his gospel; that those who commit it afterwards *hate* the Lord Jesus and his people with a fierce hatred, *curse* him in the spirit of devils, and *feel no concern of mind* about an interest in him. Then let the pastor show that in the case before him *such malignity does not exist*. To do this, he must, from previous conversation, have ascertained from the distressed himself that he would *desire*, above all things, to be interested in Christ, and that his agony springs from a belief that he is excluded from such an interest. In most such cases, *love* to the Saviour in the heart will be detected, instead of malignity. Let the pastor also recommend, with the Scriptures, the reading of such books as he judges most useful; but let him do his utmost to keep away from the troubled in mind injudicious talkers, and those who have no Christian experience.

iv. But, lastly, the mind of one may be sinking into despair in consequence of *relief being delayed*, after much seeking and importunate prayers. In such a case what must the pastor say? We reply, First. He must be careful to show the difference between pardon as the act of God, and comfort as the enjoyment of the believer, and also between faith and comfort; inasmuch as there may be great faith where there is little comfort. Second. He must inculcate that the heart of the distressed may yet have a root of bitterness in it, through pride; and therefore

more humility may be required, for "God giveth grace to the humble."
Third. He must inquire whether in all the previous seeking there has
not been too much of a self-righteous spirit and hope. Fourth. He must
teach that delays are not denials. Fifth. That delays are for the trial of
faith, hope, and patience. Sixth. That some of God's children have
waited long before they were relieved. Seventh. That we have no claim
upon God; yet, Eighth. That his promises will be fulfilled in due season.
Ninth. He must exhort to watchfulness, importunate prayer, and stead-
fast looking to Christ as our intercessor with the Father.

I have hinted that amid these spiritual troubles of the mind there
may be a *diseased nervous system* cooperating to increase dejection,
and give force to the fiery darts of the evil one. This fact must be
attended to by the pastor. He must recommend remedies for the body,
while he labors to remove burdens from the mind.

Lectures on Pastoral Theology.
Pages 236-244; 564-568.

III

Alexander McClelland, 1794-1864

Born in Scotland, Dr. McClelland came to Queen's College, and later to the seminary, from the Associate Reformed Presbytery. He taught at New Brunswick Seminary from 1832 to 1851 during a period of excitement over revivalism and "Arminianism." The sermon excerpted below, dealing with the question of encouraging the unregenerate to use the means of grace, almost involved him in a heresy trial for departing from the teachings of Dort. It is reprinted, without the introductory section, from his sermons as published in 1867.

Spiritual Regeneration Connected with the Use of Means

We call your attention in the 1st place to *the general character of his providential government of the world.* To every serious enquirer into his works and ways, the reflection must often present itself, that they are all connected with each other in the most lovely order. This stands related to *that,—that* to a third, and the union of the whole forms that golden chain which we call "divine providence or government." Hence are derived our ideas of cause and effect, antecedent and consequent, means and end. We observe certain occurrences always preceded by certain others,—and suppose the establishment of a connection between them, which we designate by various terms according to the nature of the case. As an example of the pleasure which the divinity seems to take, in linking together his works and effecting his purposes by an extended train of preliminaries, I may refer you to a class of his operations where it is impossible to discover *any* abstract propriety in the intervention of second causes. Thus when he created the heavens and the earth, he did it by a *word.* Even then, to illustrate the great principle of his government,—that of connection and dependency, he gave them a rude and chaotic existence, adorning and perfecting them by a regular process through seven days.

The same in almost all those miraculous interpositions which are recorded in the sacred page. When he visited Egypt with plagues, it was by the agency of Moses. When he stopped the sun in his course, the instrument was the prayer of his servant Joshua. When as the incarnate mediator, he went about performing deeds of miracle and mercy; he was generally pleased to associate them with some prescribed action in the subject. Hence the command to the blind man to anoint his eyes with clay; hence his usual custom of requiring the diseased to come to him and be touched. The most simple method, perhaps, of bringing creatures into the world, would be a work of immediate creation; but how different is that actually adopted. How are we preserved in being? By eating, drinking, sleeping and respiring. How do we attain that highest ornament of our nature,—knowledge? How become qualified to scan with intelligent gaze the starry concave, explore the nature of the ten thousand objects that surround us, and converse on themes for

40

angels? By commencing with a few sensible ideas—and going through an almost infinite series of preliminary exercises. On the same principle we sow and plow, and in consequence reap and eat. Before we can recline in comfort, we must have spent our waking hours in procuring a couch and covering.

But farther; if the author of nature has determined, that his blessings be only obtained in connection with certain acts or exercises on the part of his creature,—it will naturally follow, that the performance of these preliminaries must give a ground of hope that the contemplated end shall be obtained. The contrary supposition would be a libel on the goodness of the deity. Accordingly, as it is the rule of his dispensations that we always *fulfil conditions* prior to receiving,—so it appears to be equally settled that on fulfilling them, we *shall* receive. Sometimes, indeed, to display his glorious sovereignty he counteracts the best concerted enterprises, and sends the demon of disaster to blast the labors of the most persevering industry. But these, all men agree are exceptions to his ordinary system, and never to be taken as rules of conduct.— In general, the use of means secures the desired blessing.

These being the principles by which God usually regulates the communication of his favors, we may fairly ask, whether they do not create a strong presumption, that something of a similar kind will be found in the economy of grace. Why should he depart from his ordinary rule? If in the common routine of affairs, the nature of his creatures renders it proper to connect the bestowment of good with creature exercises, what is there in the concern of man's salvation to make it inexpedient here? Is it said that redemption is peculiarly of grace, and must necessarily stand opposed to human effort? This is in a measure true,— and we would admit the consequence, if it could be shewn that the doctrine of an established connection between the endeavors of the unregenerate, and the blessings of salvation attached any meritorious value to the former: but this we firmly disavow.

Some may bring forward the objection, that regeneration being the instantaneous work of the holy spirit, absolutely scorns the aid of means and preliminary exercises,—that from the nature of the case, they must be as inefficacious as food or medicine administered to the dead. I offer in reply the following observations.—Allowing the truth of the statement—what does it prove? Simply, that God has by an established law, ordained a blessing on means *in themselves inadequate* to produce the end. And what is this but a very ordinary mode of his procedure. What virtue was lodged in the clay with which Christ anointed the eyes of the blind man? What magic charm in Joshua's seven trumpets to overturn the massy ramparts of Jericho? That these prescribed antecedents had their use, we may not doubt,—but it consisted entirely in the illustration they afforded of the principle of connection and dependency.

We venture farther, and ask whether the objector will dare to say, that there is *any* second cause which may be said to have a proper efficiency in producing the effect. After all the theorising of philosophers, it is extremely doubtful whether in the idea of causation, there ought to be included (except when we apply it to the great God himself,) any thing more than *simple priority*. Let me state a familiar case, bearing a close analogy to that under consideration. The husbandman consigns a grain of wheat to the earth. Now what connection of efficiency is there between his act and the infusion of vegetable life? To answer that he *disposes* and *adapts it* for receiving the vital principle, is mere verbiage,—and can mean nothing more, than that he has placed it in those circumstances, which give reason to expect that it will be the subject of a divine operation. The infusion, however, of vegetable life in a dead seed, is a work quite as great as the communication of spiritual life to a morally dead soul, though occurring more frequently it excites less attention. Yet it must in all instances be preceded by a certain process on the part of man:—Why then in relation to the other case, may there not be a system of means provided for the sinner which secures a corresponding work of God?

But I go on to observe, that perhaps the objector is mistaken when he asserts the absence of every kind of adaptation. That unregenerate efforts exercise no proper efficiency is freely granted. But we cannot admit the absence of a relative *fitness*, which divine goodness may very properly regard in its beneficent arrangements, and which we see it *does* regard in other instances. One of the great and fundamental laws imposed on our mental constitution, is that to all our valuable acquisitions, we are led on step by step in a regular progression. By the experience of one natural principle in our bosom, we become matured for the exercise of another,—and another, and so on in an indefinite series. How easy for example, to shew that all the boasted acquirements of the sage, can be traced back to the operation of the ignoblest animal instincts! His first step was to obtain the knowledge of language. The task was soon mastered by his childish propensity to imitation. He next went to school: that which carried him there, was the instinct of filial obedience. His application to study was sustained not by literary taste, but by emulation,—sense of shame, and fear of punishment. In this manner, our various impulses and constitutional affections may be considered as so many steps appointed by the author of nature, on which his rational creatures ascend to their destined perfection: and why we ask, may not a similar plan be adopted by him in the economy of salvation? Why may we not suppose him to commence, by presenting excitement to the meaner springs of the complicated machine,—vividly impressing the sinner's imagination and lodging the seed of truth in his intellect, rousing his desires of happiness and fears of ill, his natural sense of gratitude and perceptions of moral beauty, as preparatives to the last and crowning work,—when by his spirit, he "shines into the heart and gives the light of the knowledge of the glory of himself?" In fine, may we not conclude from universal analogy, that he has established in grace, as in providence, a close connection between certain exercises on the sinner's part and a propitious agency on his own,—that consequently, faithfulness to the extent of our natural ability will secure all necessary blessings from above—on the same ground, and with the same certainty, that in common life "the hand of the diligent maketh rich."

2dly, Our conclusion rests on other grounds than analogical reasoning. It appeals to the undeniable fact, that *Jesus Christ has instituted various ordinances, the professed design of which, is the regeneration and conversion of sinners.* Such are reading the word, serious meditation, earnest prayer, and "the ministry of reconciliation." To speak of the last more particularly;—that it is intended for unregenerate men *as such,* appears evident not only from its nature, but the unambiguous command of our blessed Lord, "Go ye into all the world and preach my gospel to every creature;" "behold, I send you as sheep in the midst of wolves;" "go and teach all nations." Next to the plain terms in which this solemn commission is expressed, its best interpeter is the conduct of those entrusted with it. Now we all know how the apostles acted. They avowed themselves their master's ambassadors to pray *sinners* to be reconciled to God. Following the example of their dear Lord, who had announced that he came to seek and save that which was lost, they preached salvation to those who were *"far off,"* as well as those "who were nigh:" no extent of depravity, no darkness of understanding, no depth of unregeneracy, prevented them from washing their hands of the blood of men, by proclaiming the whole counsel of God. If the fact be so, my brethren—if Jesus Christ has instituted ordinances for the benefit of sinners as such, we infer that these have not only a right to use them, but a pledge of the divine approbation and blessing. Let none deny the conclusion who admit the premises. If the unregenerate man has instituted means of whatever kind put in his hands, we see not how it can be doubted whether the use of them to the extent of his real ability, guarantees the attainment of the end. Why were they prescribed, if they were not to be effectual; or how on this supposition can we vindicate the divine truth and wisdom?

3dly, I observe, that beside the general pledge contained in the institution of saving ordinances, *there are given explicit assurances to the diligent improver of natural principles and external aids*. Such is the exhortation of our blessed Lord in John 5, 39:—"Search the scriptures, for in them ye think ye have eternal life, and they are they which testify of me." That he was here addressing men destitute of all pretensions to a change of heart, is plain from the connection: as such, they are here treated, for the searcher of hearts cannot recognise men but in their true character. What then is the proper meaning of the exhortation? Obviously this,—that as they were rational beings, possessing natural sensibility—an approving and condemning conscience, they were immediately to engage in the investigation of divine truth, if they desired a part in that eternal life which begins in regeneration, and is consummated in glory. If it be asked whether holiness, or a right state of moral affection was not an indispensable *prerequisite;* I answer *no*,—and for the plain reason, that our Lord's design was to teach his hearers the *manner of obtaining* salvation,—of which, *holiness was an essential part*, and therefore could not be a condition. He would only have mocked his hearers, had he told them that by searching the scriptures they would obtain salvation; if in order to "search," it was necessary that they should be in a great measure saved already. This would be literally prescribing the end, as means of attaining the end. Besides,—how could these persons search the scriptures on regenerate principles, while utter strangers to divine *truth*,—that "incorruptible seed of which we are born, and which liveth and abideth forever?" The performance of the duty then, here enjoined, must be prior to a change of heart, and cannot require it as a qualification.

To the same class, we refer such exhortations as these,—"strive to enter the straight gate:" "Labor not for the meat that perisheth, but for the meat that endureth to everlasting life," "seek ye the Lord while he is to be found, call upon him while he is near." I am aware that they are generally expounded otherwise: thus we are often told that to seek God, we must exercise faith,—and repentance—and love &c.—but I cannot help thinking, that such a mode of interpretation destroys all their force and beauty. Nothing seems plainer, than that they prescribe to wretched and lost sinners *in that character*, something which is perfectly *practicable;* and the word "practicable" I use in its obvious and popular sense, applying it to actions which there is no serious difficulty in performing, without supernatural assistance. We have another objection to that gloss. If these exhortations imply the necessity of holy exercises, it will be difficult to see how they answer the purpose of exciting the sinner to use all diligence in making his calling and election sure. Will he not very naturally complain, that the preacher is blowing hot and cold upon him with one breath? He is exhorted to certain doings and efforts; but then he finds attached to them a condition which no mortal man has ever performed, without being the subject of divine agency. This he calls an *impossible* condition, and all our logic will fail to convince him of the contrary—for it is well known, that many of the learned distinctions which divines so happily employ in their contests with each other, completely elude every attempt of ordinary minds even to apprehend them. Thus circumstanced, he will probably consider it a settled point, that the exhortation cannot be addressed to *him*,—but to the highly favored children of the spirit exclusively, as they alone possess the qualifications for obedience.

It may be replied, that though obedience to the exhortation depends on divine aid, yet the unregenerate are to be urged forward on the principle, that outward performance is better than entire neglect. But is this true? Will any one say that a man, who while unrenewed in the spirit of his mind sits at the sacramental table, acts less criminally than he who under a sense of his unfitness refrains altogether? What then means the curse pronounced on unworthy partakers?—But we need not dwell on a point so evident. If any doctrine be clearly contained in the scriptures, it is, that hypocrisy or the external performance of commanded duty while stranger to appropriate dispositions, is a crime immeasurably more aggravated than the most glaring omission.

For these and other reasons, we think that the plan of identifying the exhortations referred to with the precepts of law, requiring holiness and moral perfection, is indefensible. They are not the proclamation of a stern uncompromising legislator; but the entreaties of a tender friend, and their design is to urge upon us that faithful improvement of our evangelical privileges, between which and spiritual blessing, the divine goodness has established an intimate connection. Viewed in this light, they are plain, simple, and delightfully encouraging. They subject the poor sinner to no torturing dilemmas; they require no inconsistent or impracticable conditions. They tell him that salvation is brought to his very door; and give the cheering certainty, that if he only exercise the diligence and assiduity which befits the high destiny at stake, he shall "not labor in vain nor spend his strength for nought." In a word, they are exhibitions of the same divine munificence, whose paths drop fatness on the pastures of the wilderness,—that "giveth to the beast his food, and *hears the young ravens which cry.*"

4thly, We appeal to the scriptural fact, that *diligence has in all cases been rewarded.* Sacred history is one of the best expositors of sacred truth. If, then, there was no connection between the doings of the

unregenerate and spiritual blessings, we might presume, that some examples would be recorded of a sinner falling short of salvation, after
persevering endeavors to secure it. But nothing of this kind is discovered: all the facts are decidedly on the other side of the question. Why
(to select one example from a host) was the gospel received in its love
and power by the Berean Jews, while persecuted in a neighboring city?
You reply, "because the spirit operated on their hearts." The answer is
pious and true: we only remind you, that the sacred narrative connects
his operation with something in the previous dispositions and conduct
of the persons themselves. The Bereans *were more noble than those
in Thessalonica.* Now it is certain, that the former were not regenerate
when the gospel was first preached to them:—yet there was a frankness
in their character,—an amiable docility and love of truth, which prompted
them to impartial investigation, and an honest improvement of their
religious advantages. *"Therefore,"* it is emphatically added, "many of
them believed." A clearer intimation of the principle by which God
regulates the communications of his grace, no language could give.

If an appeal be made to later experience, a thousand proofs force
themselves upon us from every side. Is it not an undeniable fact, that
wherever, in consequence of evangelical truth being preached with simplicity and fervor, or a combination of other favorable circumstances—
the minds of men are unusually stirred up from their lethargy to ask,
"what these things mean," and to make a serious business of investigat-
ing the claims of religion,—there, in the same proportion, it asserts
itself to be the "power of God unto salvation" as in apostolic times? The
benignant Paraclete seems not at all fastidious in the choice of occasions,
on which to display the riches of his goodness; nor does he refuse his
presence, when he cannot find a service as unexceptionable as that of
the seraphim round his eternal throne. He walks amidst the tumult of
a camp-meeting—overlooking every thing but the fact, that he is *invited,*
and *welcome:* that frantic vociferation so torturing to the delicate nerve,
"discourses to *his* ear excellent music:" those extravagancies which mar
the beauty of too many of our religious revivals, have not, as yet, been
found to scare him from the office which he loves. Most surely he does
not approve them: but among the tares, precious seed has been sown,
and he will not suffer it to be lost. Some may choose to think, that he
blesses only those occasions of which he himself is the first exciting
cause,—that the earnestness and desperate struggle of the soul for an
interest in saving mercy, are, without any exception, as much a part of
his special agency, as the actual renovation in which they terminate.
There is, however, no proof of this. The history of many of the excite-
ments in our day, gives little room for attributing to them a higher

origin than animal panic—curiosity—fondness for the mysterious, and
the natural love of stimulation: yet they are blest—nay we dare not
refuse to believe that in *every* instance, good has been accomplished as
lasting as eternity. In the face of almost daily observations like these—
can we doubt whether a heavenly agent is abroad among the sons of
men,—and *"waiting to be gracious?"*

Lastly, consider the tremendous charges brought against despisers of
the gospel. "And thou Capernaum," exclaimed the indignant Saviour,
"who art exalted to Heaven shall be brought down to hell: Woe unto
thee Bethsaida, for if the mighty works which are done in thee, had
been done in Tyre and Sidon, they would have repented long ago in
dust and ashes: I say, it shall be more tolerable for Tyre and Sidon in
the day of judgment than for you." The question now fairly meets us,—
wherein the sin of despising and rejecting the gospel consists: what shall
take from the impenitent hearer every plea of extenuation for his amazing folly in loving darkness rather than light? Many, perhaps, will be
disposed to rest satisfied with replying,—that though the reception of
the truth is the immediate operation of God's spirit in the soul, yet
every man has a *natural* power to believe, for the non-exercise of which,
he shall be condemned at the divine tribunal. Others, thinking this to
be an idle play of words, evading what it professes to answer, may call
to their assistance the doctrine of a federal connection between our first
parent and his posterity. According to their theory, the inability of
sinners being the fruit of crime, is itself a crime,—and they may be
justly condemned on the well known principle, that the cause is ac-
countable for all its effects. Without offering an opinion, at present, on
either of these systems,—I think it must be acknowledged, that the
doctrine which we have been advocating, is absolutely necessary to a
complete statement of the sin and inexcusableness of unbelief. We are
authorized by it to assert,—that though the moral agent cannot regenerate himself, he may procure the *grace* of regeneration; and we prove
his guilt and folly in the same way, that we prove the inexcusableness
of a man perishing for lack of food, when we tell him that by an easy
process of plowing, sowing and reaping, he would have undoubtedly
obtained it. Supposing him to object, that he could exercise no control
over the seed cast into the furrow, we should at once answer, "Thou
Fool, that is not quickened which is not *sown*; what prevented you from
placing it in a due condition for receiving the heavenly influence? Your
industrious neighbor knew as little as yourself, the mysterious art of
turning a dead kernel into a living plant: but he felt, that he was in
covenant with a bountiful parent—who, fully understood the matter,

and would send him the sunshine and the dew. In this trust he acted, and now has enough and to spare while you perish with hunger!"

Such, also, is the very language that shall be addressed to the impenitent gospel hearer. He will be distinctly told, that though the spirit alone could "work in him to will and to do," yet this spirit was as freely offered him as *atonement, pardon,* and every other covenant blessing; that by acting out his natural powers on the system of divinely appointed means, he would have as firmly secured his salvation as if it had depended on his own unassisted energies;—in fine, he will discover that God does not condemn any man *simply for unregeneracy,* but for the basest and most wanton neglect. Thus shall he be struck dumb before an assembled universe; and while he listens to the tremendous doom pronounced from the lips of eternal justice,—while he listens, foaming with agony and rancor against the most high, shall be at the same time forced to acknowledge, that "he is clear when he speaks, and righteous when he is judged."

IV

Joseph Frederick Berg, 1812-1871

The first of two J. Frederick Bergs to teach at New Brunswick, this Dr. Berg came to the Reformed Church in America from her German sister in the United States after a stormy career in opposition to the Mercersburg theology and to Roman Catholicism. Dr. Berg came to New Brunswick in 1861 when the national excitement over "nativism" and the Know Nothing party had subsided in the presence of slavery and secession, issues on which the seminary, like the denomination, seems to have said little. The rigid and unhistorical Protestantism to which anti-Romanism had driven the churches and from which Mercersburg had failed to deliver them, is illustrated in these passages from *The Old Paths* (1845). The redeeming appreciation of the irenic Heidelberg Catechism also shows forth.

The tacit acknowledgment that the Protestant Church dates its origin from the period of the reformation, has been a very common and very serious error in controverting the arrogance of the Papacy. The meaning of the title, which a large portion of the Christian church has assumed, has been perverted as much by Protestants themselves, as it has been by Papists, and the idea has been extensively diffused, that the great Christian interest, embodied and represented in the Protestant Church, is merely a Reformed Romanism. How often do we read in works treating of the reformation, the sentiment which is echoed in nine-tenths of the lectures and discourses on the same subject, that the church of Christ had become horribly corrupt; that superstition and idolatry had invaded the sanctuaries of the Most High, and the pall of darkness thick and gross had enveloped the church which Christ loved and which he purchased with his blood. The Romanist replies with exultation, "What! say you, the church of Christ had become corrupt? How can this be, when Christ has said, 'Lo I am with you alway, even unto the end of the world?' " The Protestant may frame any plea and offer any explanation, that ingenuity can devise, the argument is all on the side of his antagonist. If we admit that the Church of Rome has ever been the church of Christ, you concede the entire ground for the occupation of which, the controversy is waged. If the church of Rome was the spouse of Christ at the period of the reformation, she is and must remain the Lamb's bride to this very day. If the doctrines, forms, and usages, which are now sanctioned in the Papal Church have ever been Christian institutions, their character cannot be affected by any vicissitudes in human opinion, they must retain it to the end of the world, or the promise of the Head of the Church has proved a failure. Hence, we are shut up to a very simple alternative. The church of Rome, and by this term we mean the Papal establishment as it now is, including all its present doctrines, rites and usages, this church has either *always* been the church of Christ, or it has *never* been known or owned by the Lord. Either it is, and always has been since the period of its existence, *the apostacy*, or it is and always has been *the church*. So, on the other hand, if the Protestant Church dates its existence from the sixteenth century, it must be a schism. The doctrines and order of the Reformed Church have either been always maintained by the church of Christ, or

50

they have never been owned by the Head of the Church as the teachings
of his Spirit. It will be seen therefore, that all investigations respecting
the history of the Reformers before the reformation are replete with
intense interest. Viewed in this light, they affect the very vitals of the
body of Christ. They prove the truth of the Saviour's promise; they
show that from this ascension to the present moment, he has always
been with his church, and thus furnish ground for unshaken confidence,
that he will continue to be with her even to the end of the world. The
primary object of this sketch is to show the apostolical origin, and, in
a qualified sense, the apostolical succession of the Reformed Church.
We do not intend to erect a fabric of bigotry or exclusiveness upon the
ground which we claim. Far be it from us to maintain that none can
prove their title to the Christian name unless they establish their immediate relation to the Presbyterian family. God forbid. We do insist,
however, that every recent phase of Protestantism is a branch of the old
Waldensian stem, whose roots are imbedded in apostolic ground.

We have another design in calling attention to the order and discipline
of the ancient Reformed Church. We wish to encourage the spirit of
inquiry respecting the "old paths," and to examine the landmarks which
the ancients have set. The Christians of the eleventh as well as of the
sixteenth and intervening centuries, were more fiercely assailed by persecution than the disciples of any age subsequent to the apostolical and
primitive eras. Their blood was poured out like water, but they continued firm and faithful unto death. They loved their church, and they
were ready to fill up that which was behind of the afflictions of Christ,
and to go with their Lord and Master to the cross, the gallows and the
stake, to prison and to death. We venerate their memory; we bless God
for their constancy, and we would inquire what was the order of their
churches, what was their mode of indoctrinating their youth and instill-
ing into the minds of the common people this unquenchable love for
the scriptures, long before the art of printing was invented. Perhaps,
with our superior advantages, we may profit both by their precept and
example, and find that they understood quite as fully as the men of this
generation all that is essential to the profession and maintenance of the
life and power of pure and undefiled religion.

The symbol of the protestant faith has always been THE BIBLE—and
wherever the essential doctrines of Christianity have obtained only a
partial hold upon the sympathies of a community, there has always been
a readiness to meet upon this common ground, and to spread broad-
cast over the land the open Bible, without note or comment, as the
greatest and best charter of human rights which Heaven has ever bestowed upon men; and, on the other hand, wherever the principles of

popery have gained sufficient strength to venture upon the development
of its prime peculiarities, the very first indication of the real character
of the papal system has always and every where been displayed in the
most strenuous, bitter, and unrelenting, yet often artful and specious
assaults upon the exercise of this privilege of universal access to the
pages of the Bible. You may illustrate this truth by the history of Rome's
policy towards the scriptures, in every age, and in every country, since
the establishment of the papal despotism. From the tenth to the sixteenth century, the period which includes what may well be denominated the dark ages, and from the sixteenth down to the nineteenth
century, Rome's hatred against the Bible has been written in characters
of fire and blood. Witness the sufferings of the Lollards in England—
read the narrative of the persecutions of the Scotch and Irish martyrs—
consult the annals of the Waldensian brethren—read the history of the
reformation in Germany and Switzerland—view the struggles of the
Huguenots in France—look at the suppression of the protestant faith
in Spain—in Italy—and every where you read in authorized decrees of
the church of Rome, (as binding upon the consciences of papists to-day,
as ever they were,) the most unrelenting and implacable hostility against
the people's right to read the scriptures in their own language.—Extend
your view to the present age, and you find that not many years ago, the
pope of Rome in an official bull, or letter, declared that Bible societies
were "inventions of the devil." Call to mind a few of the facts with which
the experience of the last three years has made us all familiar. What
means the agitation in New York and in Philadelphia respecting the use
of the Bible in public schools? Why has the entire population of our
country, from Maine to Florida, been excited by the question?—which
is not yet fully decided—though it will, probably, ere long be for ever
settled—whether our children may read the scriptures, as their fathers
have hitherto done, without let or hindrance, restriction, or dictation,
from the vassals of the pope of Rome? Do we not know that in most of
the wards in the city of New York, during the late popish ascendency,
the reading of the Bible was entirely dispensed with? and that, so far
as the public schools were concerned, it was a forbidden book, as completely as though the fourth rule of the index expurgatory had been
adopted, by the civil authorities, as the law of the land? Have we not
heard of the sacrilegious burning of two hundred copies of the holy
scriptures, in the northern part of the state of New York? In open day,
with shouts of exultation, the protestant Bible was hurled, by the priests
of Rome, into the flames!—These things have not been done in a corner,
and we mention them now, as collateral, and by no means irrelevant
testimony in favour of the principle which we have stated, that the

respective esteem in which the book of God has been held, in all ages and countries, has been the grand criterion by which popery and protestantism have always been distinguished.

The principal symbolical book in the reformed church, is the Heidelberg catechism, a work of great celebrity in the history of the reformation, and a most admirable compend of Christian doctrine. It was prepared by order of Frederic III., elector of the Palatinate, and was first published A.D. 1563. The principal contributors were Ursinus, professor of theology in the Heidelberg university, and Olevianus, a minister and public teacher at the same place. The main design in the framing of the catechism was to present the great truths of the Christian faith in such a manner that all really evangelical minds might harmonize in the statement, and this important object has been gained. The Heidelberg catechism has been translated into many languages, and is regarded with favour by denominations of Christians who differ widely on many points of doctrine. It is believed that it can be rejected by none excepting those who repudiate the essentials of Christianity. The sound, scriptural, and clear expositions of divine truth, which it presents, render it a most desirable text-book for the instruction of youth, and its use in sabbath schools and Bible classes cannot be too strongly recommended. The German Reformed Church in this country acknowledges no other symbolical book, and it has hitherto been found amply sufficient as an exponent of the faith professed in our communion. Of course, the Bible has precedence over every other book; the object of confessions of faith is not to divert attention from the teachings of God's holy word, but so to arrange its doctrines and truths that the various parts of the system shall be shown in their mutual relations, that thus the study and apprehension of the doctrines of the gospel may be facilitated. The cry which is commonly heard in some sections against all creeds, need not alarm the weakest Christian. If isolated instances can be shown in which undue regard has been paid to these human compositions, or in which they have been exalted above the lively oracles of God, thousands and tens of thousands are ready, in our own day, to stand forth and testify that their use has been more advantageous to them than the alleged abuse could have been hurtful to those who are supposed to have been injured by them. So far from leading the mind away from God's truth as revealed in his word, the Heidelberg catechism renders the searching of the scriptures absolutely indispensable, every answer being framed in scriptural language, and containing numerous references to the lively oracles of God in support of every doctrine which is advanced. If the members of our churches would introduce this little book into their families, and restore the good old custom of teaching their children, on the afternoon of the Lord's day, the lessons of the catechism, they would be laying a foundation upon which, with God's blessing, it would be easy to build, in subsequent life. A clear apprehension of the system of Christian doctrine presented in the Heidelberg catechism will tend powerfully to fortify the mind against the novelties and heresies by which the devil is constantly seeking to corrupt the minds of our youth, and by pre-occupying the ground, render it almost impossible for the enemy to introduce his tares. It is worth while to inquire amongst what classes of men and professing Christians, the Miller and Mormon delusions and *eruptions* of that kind have made the greatest progress. So far as private observation has extended, converts to such idle dreams are made principally from among the ignorant and the feebleminded, such as have never enjoyed opportunities in their youth of becoming indoctrinated in the truths of the gospel, and who have been virulent in their denunciations of all creeds and confessions; or whose religion has, in short, been that of the imagination and the passions, and not of the heart.

To deny that the catechism of the reformed church has been greatly perverted in very many instances, would be wicked as well as useless, and we trust we shall not be understood as contending for a revival or continuance of any such abuse. We are all persuaded that the mere acquaintance with the catechism, the simple memorising of its questions and answers, is not a sufficient preparation for church membership; its use for such a purpose ought not to be countenanced; but, in all cases, there should be strict and earnest inquiry respecting the personal experience of the candidate, and if the applicant for admission to sealing ordinances has no evidence, and professes to have no evidence of a change of heart, the door should be barred against his introduction to the fellowship of the church. But, whilst this will be generally admitted, we maintain that the instruction of the youth of our churches in accordance with our symbolical book, their indoctrination, has been a cherished instrumentality in the hands of many a faithful minister, by means of which, multitudes now in glory have been led to the knowledge of the truth which has made them free, and have, through divine grace, become wise unto salvation. We believe that there is a general disposition to restore the catechism to the place which properly belongs to it, even among those who, from their knowledge of the abuse to which it has been subjected, have heretofore been disposed to regard it with a degree of suspicion and prejudice. The church of the Palatinate, to which the honour pertains of furnishing this excellent compendium, took special pains to provide for its explanation to both young and old, and made it part of the ministerial labour to frame at least one discourse on the Sabbath with peculiar reference to some portion of its contents, and we are prepared to acquiesce in this regulation as judicious.

As regards the doctrine of our symbolical book, it may be stated as decidedly though moderately Calvinistic. It certainly is not Arminian; and, although it is silent on many of the vexed questions of theology, its whole tenor is such as to guard against the errors in theory and practice, which a rejection of the doctrines of grace naturally develops. Whilst the German Reformed Church in this country, can claim as pure and scriptural a standard as any orthodox denomination in the world, her position in this country is that of a mediator between members of the Calvinistic family who are divided on points of minor importance, which belong, properly to the philosophy of religion; whilst insisting upon the great truths which are essential to the maintenance of the faith of the gospel, she affords a latitude on other questions which involve less important principles. This is a necessary result of her adherence to the Heidelberg catechism as her only symbol, which, as already remarked, was framed with a view to Christian compromise.

The Old Paths.
Pages viii-xii, 30-32, 182-186.

V

John VanNest Talmage, 1819-1892

A member of the class of 1845, Dr. Talmage was a missionary in China
from 1847 to 1892. He was active in evangelism, opposition to the opium
trade, the preparation of Christian literature and in many other ways.
From his diary and letters, as published in John G. Fagg's *Forty Years
in South China*, we get some vivid pictures of the ideals and concepts
of the missionary movement of that period.

From *Forty Years in South China*

"Independent of the reproach which the opium traffic casts on the Christian religion, we find it a great barrier in the way of evangelizing this people. We cannot put confidence in an opium smoker. A man who smokes it in even the smallest degree we should not dare to admit into the Christian church. More than one-half of the men at Amoy are more or less addicted to the habit. Of this half of the population the missionary can have comparatively but little hope. We know the grace of God can deliver from every vice and there have been examples of reformation even from this. Yet from experience when talking to an opium smoker we always feel discouraged. Although this be a discouraging feature in our operations here, it should only be a stimulus to the Church to send more laborers and put forth greater efforts to stem the tide of destruction which the Christian world is pouring in upon the heathen. Independent of the principles of benevolence, justice demands of Christendom that the evil be stayed, and reparation if possible be made for the injury already done. If nothing more, let there be an equivalent for what has been received from China. It is a startling fact, that the money which Christian nations have received from China for this one article, an article which has done to the Chinese nothing but incalculable injury, far, far exceeds all the money which has been expended by all Protestant churches on all Protestant missions in all parts of the heathen world since the days of the Reformation.

ROMANIZED COLLOQUIAL

"The question whether there is any way by which this people can be made a reading people, especially by which the Christians may be put in possession of the Word of God, and be able to read it intelligently for themselves, has occupied much thought of the missionaries here. At present most of the church members have no reading for the Sabbath and for private meditation. They may have family worship, but they cannot at their worship read the Holy Scriptures. Some of us are now trying an experiment whether by means of the Roman alphabet the

Sacred Scriptures and other religious books may not be given to the
Christians and to any others who cannot read, but who take enough of
an interest in Christianity to desire to read the Scriptures for themselves.
By the use of seventeen of these letters we can express every consonant
and vowel sound in the Amoy dialect, and by the use of a few additional
marks we can designate all the tones. Dr. James Young, an English
Presbyterian missionary physician, has commenced teaching the colloquial, as written with the Roman alphabet, in his school, a school formerly under the care of Mr. Doty. From his present experience he is
of opinion that boys who are at all apt in acquiring instruction, in less
than three months may be prepared for reading the Scriptures, with
understanding. I have a class of three or four adults an hour an evening
four evenings in the week, receiving instruction in the colloquial. They
have taken some half dozen lessons and are making good progress. At
present we have no printed primers or spelling-books, and are compelled to teach principally by blackboard. We are of opinion that almost
every member of the church can soon learn to read by this system.
Arrangements have been made to print part of the history of Joseph in
colloquial. These are but experiments. If they succeed according to our
present hope, it may be worth while to have the whole Bible and other
religious books printed in this manner. A little more experience will
enable us to speak with more confidence for or against the plan."

CHINESE SENSE OF SIN

"I think the Chinese are very different in their religious feelings from
many other (perhaps from the most of other) heathen people. We have
often heard of the great sacrifices which the heathen of India will make
and the great sufferings they will impose on themselves in order to
make atonement for their sins and appease the anger of the gods. There
may occasionally be something of the kind among the Buddhists of
China. But I rather suppose that where there are any self-mortifications
imposed (which is very rare in this part of China), they are imposed to
secure merit, not to atone for sin. I do not remember ever to have met
with an individual among the Chinese who had any sense of sinfulness
of heart, or even any remorse for sinfulness of conduct except he was
first taught it by the Gospel. It is one of the most difficult truths to
convey to their minds that they are sinners against God. We have had
a few inquirers who have expressed a deep sense of sinfulness. But this
sense of sinfulness has come from hearing the Gospel. The way the
most of those, whom we doubt not are true Christians, have been led

on seems to be as follows: They hear the Gospel, presently they become convinced of its truth. Their first impulses then seem to be those of joy and gratitude. They are like men who were born blind, and had never mourned over their blindness, because they had no notion of the blessing of sight. Presently their eyes begin to be opened and they begin to see. They only think of the new blessings which they are receiving, not of the imperfections which still remain in their vision. A sense of these comes afterwards. Was not this sometimes the case in the days of the Apostles? It was not so on the day of Pentecost. The multitude were 'pricked in their hearts' because the moment they were convinced that Jesus was the Christ they were filled with a sense of their wickedness in crucifying Him. So it is with persons in Christian lands when their minds become interested in the truth; they are made to feel their wickedness in so long resisting its influences. But the case seems to have been different when Philip first carried the Gospel to Samaria. The first effect there seems to have been that of 'great joy.'

"It seems to be thus in Amoy. The conviction of deep sinfulness comes by meditating on the Gospel, the work of Christ, etc.

"It is the doctrine of the cross of Christ, after all, which should be the theme of our discourses."

BREAKING AND BURNING OF IDOLS

"Feb. 27, 1848. To-day an old lady and her two sons declared themselves to be worshippers of Jesus by presenting their idols to Bro. Pohlman. On the evening of the last day of their last year they had burnt their ancestral tablets. It was an interesting sight, said Bro. Pohlman, to see the old lady, supported by one of her sons, breaking her idols and making a voluntary and public surrender of them at the chapel.

"March 1st. When the old lady returned from the chapel on Sunday evening she was full of zeal, and began preaching to her neighbors on the folly of idolatry. She was so successful that another old lady living in the same house with her has made a bonfire and burned all her idols except one. This, being made of clay, was not combustible. This she presented to Pohlman to-day. He asked her whether she gave it up willingly. She said she rejoiced to do it. She said she had not yet destroyed her ancestral tablets. Pohlman told her he did not wish her to do it rashly. She must reflect on the subject, and when she became convinced that the worship of them was a sin against God she must give them up immediately."

Letters and journal quoted by John G. Fagg in
Forty Years in South China, pages 104-109, 83.

VI
John De Witt, 1821-1906

A member of the class of 1842, Dr. De Witt taught in the seminary from 1863 to 1892. He was prominent in the preparation and publication of the American Standard Version of the Bible (1901). His *What Is Inspiration?* (1893) is perhaps, given its time, the most significant piece of theological writing produced by New Brunswick Theological Seminary, combining a firm evangelical faith with the insights of historical criticism and evolutionary thought.

From *What Is Inspiration?*

REVELATION KEEPING PACE WITH DEVELOPMENT

WHILE we are yet thinking of God as revealing himself to men, we must not leave unconsidered the co-ordinate and proportional advance, as in living unison, of the principle and its product, of the cause and the effect. The divine manifestation and the human apprehension move forward together toward a goal in the future,—the perfected Christ of the Gospels, reproduced in the lives of men.

By a persistence of the original energy a historic revelation increases in clearness and efficiency, and this with distinct reference to the growth of its recipients in knowledge and grace, growth ever stimulating growth.

How like this is to the advance, from stage to stage, and from form to form, in the sphere of nature since the first creative act! What name shall we give to the principle or law that connects all phenomena, spiritual and physical, with other preceding phenomena in which they apparently, and in some respects really, originate,—although not by any causation that operates independently of the immediate, immanent presence and pressure of the divine will? Thus carefully guarded, there is no better term than that which modern science has chosen, and might have caught up from the creative account in Genesis, with its *births* or *generations* of successive typical forms, as expressed by a familiar Hebrew word, which always implies *parentage*. The term *evolution*, although less graphic than the Hebrew conception *birth*, describes admirably the principle manifested, not only in the material universe, but in God's self-revelation, in all that addresses itself to the mind, as including all intellective and reasoning faculties, in the *natural* sphere; and also to the heart, the conscience, the will, the affections, and all organs of a highly spiritual nature, in the *moral* sphere.

The writer of these pages is a believer, and ever more intelligently and thoroughly a believer, in a divine principle of evolution. He sees it in the wide and varied outspread of nature, and in all the activities of natural law. For what is natural law, but the human conception of divine and orderly action? He sees it, not only in rocks, with their fossil remains of vegetable and animal life, but in language, in history, in science, in religion—in things in the heavens and things in the earth—

61

above, beneath, around, everywhere—and so, with the rest, in the
revelation of God in the Bible.

It is Herbert Spencer's idea—a magnificent generalization. As expressed by the philosopher it is lamentably deficient, in failing to recognize distinctly the omnipotent, personal God immanent in nature, as
its animating and impelling energy. With this indispensable correction,
we accept it in principle, with whatever variation in details.

The living personal God is the centre and source of all life, of all
organic development, of all advance to more perfect modes of existence,
processes, and functions. Nothing is out of his reach and grasp, nothing
too great or too insignificant for the exercise of his power. The infinite
Spirit in his wise and loving activities is behind the scene. He that was,
and is, and shall be—ὁ ἐρχόμενος, *the coming one*—is ever coming
out more manifestly from the depths of his infinite nature, infusing
himself into, and impressing himself upon, everything that through his
will exists. He ever progressively and more distinctly unfolds himself
before those who have eyes to see; and so is ever educating their eyes
to see more clearly whatever, as his scheme develops, he may yet have
to show them.

In this moving, changeful exposition, the grand panorama of all that
may be known among men, God, working from within outwardly, is
the Exhibitor, wisely adapting the exposition in its breadth and contents
to the ever-growing capacity to which it is addressed. Man, the spec-
tator, as well as, in his generations, a principal component in the exhibition, ever beholding more appreciatively, and becoming more deeply
interested in the unceasing progressing, onward and still onward.

DISCRIMINATIVE DEFINITION

But in impressing a moral lesson by historic incident, in reaching the
conscience, in moving the deeper religious sensibilities which stimulate
and energize the will—which we have found to be the principal
purpose of the revelation of God in the Scriptures—verbal inspiration
could not be required. As for moral impression by historic statement,
fiction is nearly as good as fact, or we should have no parables. For any
ordinary use, the honest effort to ascertain the facts, and their statement
with truthful purpose, is accepted as sufficient, even if some minor
details are thought doubtful.

Our examination of the contents of the Bible in their diversity, and
of the great variety of circumstances and characteristics of human existence to which they relate, has prepared us for a definition less com-

pact, rigid, and inflexible than those which Systematic Theology usually
requires and produces.

The inflexible definitions that confine the infinite Spirit of God within
our narrow human measurements,—saying to him, Thus far shalt thou
go, and no farther,—are to be studiously avoided. He is ever transcend-
ing the limitations we assign to him, casting off the trammels, asserting
his liberty in the most practical way, and putting our sagacity to shame.

The following definition is intentionally copious. It has been made so
comprehensive as to include the whole concrete result of inspiration
exhibited in the Sacred Books, that is, the whole content and substance
of Biblical Theology. Having the material spread out before us in its
amplitude, it may be easy for any one so inclined to reduce its dimen-
sions by omitting whatever he thinks least important to strict definition,
in accordance with the tendency of the more scholastic theological systems to philosophical abstraction. But the practical design of this essay
carries us in the opposite direction.

*Inspiration is a special energy of the Spirit of God upon the mind
and heart of selected and prepared human agents which does not obstruct nor impair their native and normal activities, nor miraculously
enlarge the boundaries of their knowledge, except where essential to the
inspiring purpose; but stimulates and assists them to the clear discernment and faithful utterance of truth and fact, and when necessary
brings within their range truth or fact which could not otherwise have
been known. By such direction and aid, through spoken or written
words, in combination with any divinely ordered circumstances with
which they may be historically interwoven, the result contemplated in
the purpose of God is realized in a progressive revelation of his wisdom,
righteousness, and grace for the instruction and moral elevation of men.
The revelation so produced is permanent and infallible for all matters
of faith and practice; except so far as any given revelation may be
manifestly partial, provisional, and limited in its time and conditions,
or may be afterwards modified or superseded by a higher and fuller
revelation, adapted to an advanced period in the redemptive process to
which all revelation relates as its final end and glorious consummation.*

It is on the *a posteriori* principle that we have been working. In the
preceding chapters we have attempted a survey of the whole ground,
noting the characteristic phenomena of the collection of books called
Holy Scripture, referring to the salient points and most remarkable
facts, and at last summed them up in what we have now given. There
is not a point that had not been provided for in the preceding exhibit.

Yet full as the definition is, it needs supplementing, and the supple-
ment also has been anticipated. It lies very near, and we must have it

if we would understand the subject in its breadth, and must use it for our final relief. Confusion might result from an endeavor to include it in the same formula. Its proper place is close alongside, where we can pass easily from one to the other. We shall find our way to it presently.

The above definition in its reference to "progressive revelation" and human development, is intended to provide for disclosures of truth suited to the stage of moral and spiritual growth that had been reached when it was made. The inspiring energy did not confer omniscience, and did not lift its subjects so far above the plane of thought that characterized their age as to be out of touch with it.

Our conception admits that together with the clearer apprehension and higher moral tone that resulted from the supernatural quickening of his faculties, enabling the prophet at times to discover truth before unrevealed, a commingling of human misconception was suffered to remain till the time should come for further disclosure. The revelation that could at first be apprehended by human capacity was of a very low grade. As imperfectly appropriated, it might give rise to deeds of loyalty to the divine will, expressing savage detestation of heathenism, that seem shocking to us, and impossible to reconcile with the highest moral excellence. This is the revelation which the definition refers to as "partial, provisional, and limited to its own time." Of the test by which this may be determined we shall speak presently.

It is often asserted most positively in controversy with those who refer discriminatively to different parts of the Bible, assigning a higher value to the later than to the earlier revelation, that the Old Testament, as well as the New, is perfect and infallible in its minutest details. The highest inspiration is claimed equally for every part. But who can say intelligently, in this sweeping sense, that the entire Bible, for all time is "the perfect and infallible rule of faith and practice," or any one Book in the Old Testament? To press this familiar statement from the Confession against those who find serious imperfections in the earlier Scriptures, is mere jugglery of words. No one who uses it against others as condemnatory, believes it himself of the Old Testament apart from the New. If we would avoid confusion of thought, nothing is more important than reasonable discrimination.

THE DEFINITION COMPLETED AND THE FINAL TEST

We shall not have fulfilled our proposed task until we have reached a satisfactory conclusion for disturbed minds with regard to the varying degrees of certainty in the Bible which the foregoing definition assumes.

This may mean, in the estimation of many, uncertainty everywhere, interminable perplexity whenever they open the Bible.

They may feel obliged to accept our conclusions, as apparently founded on a correct view of its character and contents. Nevertheless they are distressed, and almost wish they had been left in their previous contentment. They had supposed it was all holy ground, and they might plant their foot firmly in all its borders. But now they shall fear quagmires and quicksands at every step. The thought of this is almost enough to engulf them in John Bunyan's allegorical *Slough of Despond.* Even a "Thus-saith-the-Lord" seems to be no guarantee against principally human derivation, and a consequent impairment of the divine thought. This is even worse than impairment by copyists or translators. "Where are we," they ask, "and where, if anywhere, shall we find safety?"

We should not have commenced this work, if we could not, anticipating such questions, have furnished a reply that shall more than renew their former confidence. While we have appeared to be doing harm, we shall have done immeasurable good.

Is there anything in the Bible,—it seems a strange question, but we must ask it,—that is not inspired? We do not refer to language attributed to Satan or to evil-minded men. There is plenty of that. But look in the opposite direction. Are there statements or communications *superior* to anything to be thought of as inspired? If we hesitate, he that now speaketh to us from heaven himself shall give answer, and his words are faithful and true: "*Whosoever drinketh of the water that I shall give him shall never thirst; but the water that I shall give him shall become in him a well of water springing up unto eternal life.*"

Is it asked again, "How shall I find my way to the fountain of truth, that drinking I may live forever?" Again the answer—this also is in the first person singular, and is decisive: "*I am the way, and the truth, and the life; no one cometh to the Father but through me.*"

We are now ready for an emphatic statement, supplementary to our definition. It was not long enough.

No proposed definition of God's inspiring grace can be accepted as complete unless it has been formulated (1) in the light of the grand central truth in which inspiration and revelation alike culminate, that Jesus Christ as a person, "the Only-begotten of the Father," is the final, perfect, and the only perfect revelation of God to men; and (2) with due regard to the radical difference between the words of Christ, who is himself the truth, and those of all inspired teachers, as between the primary and every secondary source of divine knowledge and authority.

To this must be added a companion sentence that leads us one step further in the attempted reconstruction. Both have been provided for in preceding chapters.

(1) *All historic, prophetic, and didactic revelation of God in the inspired Books of the Old and New Testaments, is inferior and subordinate to his revelation of personal truth and grace in the Christ of the historic Gospels; and (2) whatsoever the former may contain that is incongruous therewith, whatever be the explanation of the incongruity, is not to be held as authoritative for us, but is virtually superseded, as an imperfect and provisional inspiration.*

Shall we put one more question growing out of the uncertainty of merely human sources, even if inspired, and test his ability to answer? There can be no jugglery here. We have found one who can probe the depths of our hearts, while he reveals to us the heart of God. We may ask confidently:

How may one know beyond doubt that the words of Christ recorded in the Gospels actually contain the living truth he is in search of?

The ready answer comes, and indeed it is probing: *"He that will do his will shall know the teaching, whether it be of God, or whether I have spoken of myself."*

It depends, then, upon ourselves, and suggests the heart-searching question, Do I give myself up absolutely to the control of God, sincerely desiring to do his will, if I may only know it? Then shall we know the truth, and shall be prepared to say, "Lord, to whom shall we go? thou hast the words of eternal life, and we believe and know that thou art the Christ, the Son of the living God."

If this surrender is thorough and unreserved, our trouble is ended. No clouds and darkness henceforth—no fog-banks intercepting the divine light—no quicksands and quagmires. We go forward with unfaltering step. We shall walk in the light as God is in the light, shall have fellowship one with another, and the blood of Jesus his Son cleanseth us from all sin. Verily we have found an highway, a royal road, on which the sun always shines. It leads up to "the city whose gates are of pearl, and its streets of pure gold, and which hath no need of the sun, neither of the moon to shine upon it, for the glory of God doth lighten it and the Lamb is the light thereof."

The riddles that have embarrassed us shall all be solved now, or those which we cannot or need not solve, we shall be able to cast aside as frivolous, or will class them with "the secret things that belong unto the Lord our God," and be perfectly content. It is all in his hands, and some things we can take upon trust. Enough for us that in all matters of importance our doubts shall be dissipated forever.

We have made above, somewhat separately, two points that are of the first importance and ever to be remembered. The *first* is, that he who came from heaven to identify himself with men gave his personal assurance that his words should be correctly reported. Through his Holy Spirit, the revealer of truth, he would look after this matter himself. The *second* is, that he ascribed to his own words a special potency, a spirit and life, by which they should be distinguished to the inmost consciousness of him who receives them in humble faith, from all others. They should be a revelation of the Son of God within him. Their spirit and life should become elements in his being, enabling him to say, "It is no longer I that live, but Christ liveth in me; and the life which I now live in the flesh, I live by faith, the faith which is of the Son of God, who loved me, and gave himself for me."

We reverse, then, the usual order of suggestion, for those who are painfully anxious to know whether in this Bible we have the saving word of God. We do not ask a man to satisfy himself by careful study with innumerable preliminaries in an older revelation, some of which are adapted to times and circumstances into which we cannot transport ourselves, the nature and needs of which we cannot comprehend, and which have suffered we know not how much from the ravages of time, and the ignorance or presumption of men, sometimes pious and well-meaning. What care we for such a revelation, although otherwise of immense interest and value, in comparison with "the light of the knowledge of the glory of God in the face of Jesus Christ" as we now gaze upon it? We have found him of whom Moses and the prophets wrote, we hear his words, and in them we discover the heart of God as our Almighty Father and everlasting Friend. We know the truth, and it has made us free indeed, and free forever.

In this conviction we are ready now for the Old Testament. We may be reasonably asked by any inquirer after truth, If the Bible was given by inspiration of the Spirit, and contains great thoughts of God, of imperishable value, and yet is full of imperfections, how shall I discriminate between the better and the worse? If, besides the divine truth that it embodies, it also contains partial truths, which are sometimes as misleading as falsehood, and moral incongruities and monstrosities from which our souls recoil, how shall I separate the gold from the dross? By the use of my reason? Would you have me become a rationalist?

Yes, rather than be a sophist or a simpleton. Yes, a thousand times, if one becomes a rationalist by making use of his reason, including conscience and every spiritual faculty with which God has endowed him, strengthened and enlightened by the word, and life, and spirit of Christ. Who will fling a gibe at us for such rationalism—a rationalism that verges so closely upon inspiration?

This is the final and decisive test of all utterances or writings known among men. Having the principal, central, all-embracing truth embedded in our hearts, "we have an unction from the Holy One and know all things." We go fearlessly, therefore, to the old inspiration, approving or rejecting, as it may be. If anything agrees not with these words of Christ in the Gospels, and with the life of God incarnate, as illustrating his words,—no matter how it came to be what it is, no matter to whose ignorance and hardness of heart it may have been adaptively lowered,—polygamy, slavery, revenge, and barbarity of every kind,—we renounce and denounce it as evil. Our enlightened moral instinct rejects it unreservedly and forever. Any disciple of Christ that does not speak according to this word knows not what spirit he is of. Let him come closer to Christ in his pervasive, effluent, and communicative moral purity. Let him take John's position, pillowing his head on the Master's bosom, where he can hear his faintest whisper and feel every throb of his pure, tender, and loving heart, and he will come to a better mind.

Yes, this is the final and decisive test, from which there can be no appeal to a higher court, and we offer it as a relief from all difficulty, as respects the principal point we have considered. We reaffirm unfalteringly our proposition, as the most incontestable of moral axioms, that *whatsoever in the Old Testament revelation, or in any professed revelation from God, is not in accord with the revelation of his righteousness, or purity, or love, or truth, in the words and life of Christ, has been annulled and superseded, and is practically no revelation for us.*

There can be no modification of this sweeping judgment. It must stand for all time, challenging disproof or contradiction. Yet any reasonable relief that may be possible shall be cheerfully accorded. We must not be misunderstood for a moment. And therefore an emphatic restatement of earlier thought may be suffered together with some additions.

It is not the mutilation of the Bible that we suggest, as if all enormities should be stricken from the record of fact. Even for us they have their moral uses, if only by repulsion, as we contrast them with the higher law and the purer morality under which we are living.

They have also severally their historic accompaniment, which relieves some of their worst features. If we sit in judgment, in any given instances upon record, upon the *men*, whose thoughts and practices were so far below the standard that has been prescribed for our own regulation that we instinctively reprobate them, our judgment must be mitigated by important extenuating circumstances, which are righteously considered in every court of justice before sentence is pronounced. These circumstances may impart a different aspect both to their own conduct and to the divine rule under which was permitted the moral evil that shocks us. Every special transaction that comes under review is part of an extended narrative. It has its background, and its foreground,—a lower morality in the past, and a higher in the future.

This semi-barbarous people had their moral law. Whatever may have been its imperfections, it was gradually but surely regenerative. It was educating their conscience, although on account of their depressed moral status in a very rude way. They were in a low form in the school of their divine Teacher, but they were in, and not outside of, his school. They were being taught that men were so far above the brutes that they could recognize a personal God. They enjoyed the dignity of being persons. They were also learning that they were morally responsible,—that there were some things that they might not do without incurring the displeasure of their Lawgiver.

And further, if a command issued by a divinely appointed leader is intolerably repulsive to us, it was not so to *them*. We who have attained higher forms in the world-wide schoolroom of the great Instructor of men, may find occasion in these narratives to bless him for the results of his wise, pure, and faithful teaching, in the moral sensibilities that stir our hearts when we read what horrid things were done by those of our own race only a few centuries ago, without a thought of their being evil.

The men whose lives we are contemplating with aversion were on the ascending grade. They were in the firm grasp of one who was bearing the race they represented forward and upward. The results of his teaching will appear further on, and its wisdom and effectiveness will be fully justified.

Take for example the butcheries in Canaan under Joshua. A little while before their historic time, those who committed them, like those they exterminated as wild beasts, would have performed such cruelties for cruelty's sake. But now, conscience was being exercised. This was quite a new thing in the earth. There could have been no such lessons inculcated in the school of Moloch, Baal, or Astarte. As reasons for the act, they were told of the gross corruptions to which these people were addicted. The subsequent extermination was not the wanton and unmitigated barbarity it must otherwise have been. They were taught practically to detest as horrible and hateful the forms of wickedness that were branded as evil in their own law.

It is true that lessons of the sacredness of human life, and of tenderness, pity, and brotherly-kindness with which we are so familiar, were strikingly absent here. But these were among the advanced lessons of the future, which should at last purge the earth from all its wickedness.

Give them time. From the nature of the case everything cannot be done at once for men in the moral degradation and imperviousness to right impressions from which they were gradually being rescued.

We thus see what deep and far-reaching principles lie here. Do not mutilate the Book, nor expunge even a single page. It may not be very pleasant reading—quite the opposite. But if we study it carefully, the foulest record has its indirect moral uses for all the world. It would be a miserably superficial thought,—no one in his right senses would entertain it,—that because such things were done several thousand years ago under apparent divine sanction, they were morally right. We are not to call evil *good*, nor good *evil*, because something on the surface of the Bible in early times of moral stupidity seems to obliterate moral distinctions.

There might be in the divine rule some temporary accommodation to hardness of heart, in view of the fact that softening influences were at work. But bad is bad, all the world over and for all time, and it never can be good. We must not suffer the moral sensitiveness that is the greatest glory of our nature, and which under the teaching of Christ is becoming exquisitely true and sound in its judgments, to become blunted by such records of far-off facts and ethical conditions different from our own.

Let it be conceded that a long time ago God mercifully "overlooked" some things that are unspeakably evil. Yet he now commands all men everywhere to repent of and abjure them. Thank God that we have become so sensitive to such evil that we shrink from it with wondering horror through the teaching and example of our blessed Savior and the grace of his transforming Spirit.

We take, then, an enlightened view of the divine government under the mysteries that formerly enwrapped it. We can look with some leniency at these men of old,—savage, yet human like ourselves. Such might we have been but for God's grace. But when we have regard to the *evil itself*, apart from these extenuating considerations, we condemn it unsparingly as its moral enormity deserves. The ruling that permitted it still stands, as part of the record of irreversible facts. But we now judge of this ruling by a later and more perfect divine revelation. As respects the regulation of our own lives, the former is abolished and superseded. The holy light in which we live reveals the true character of the deeds here described, and for our thought and practice such Scripture has no authority. Moral offences so unspeakably evil, we repel and detest under the higher law and illumination of Christ. That they are in the Bible need not trouble us in the least.

We repeat then with emphasis our axiom, and without abatement:

*Whatsoever in the Old Testament revelation, or in any professed reve-
lation from God, is not in accord with the righteousness, or love, or
purity, or truth, in the words and the life of Christ, has been annulled
and superseded, and is practically no revelation for us.*

The errancy of Scripture disturbs us no more. Christ himself is our
pattern and law, which can never fail us. The all-perfect revelation of
the glory of God in the person, life, and instructions of our divine
Redeemer, is like the electric search-light so important in our modern
naval warfare. It dissipates all darkness, and exposes to detestation
everything contrary to God and his law in thought, or word, or deed.

What Is Inspiration?
Pages 96-99, 162-169, 178-185.

VII

Ferdinand Schureman Schenck, 1845-1925

A member of the class of 1872, Dr. Schenck was professor of practical theology from 1899 to 1924. His published works reveal an acceptance of the evolutionary thought that was to cause much excitement toward the end of that period. Further, he shared with his colleague, John De Witt, an equal appreciation of the importance of the social questions that were beginning to concern serious thinkers. The first of the following selections is from *Christian Evidences and Ethics* (1910); the others from *The Sociology of the Bible* (1909).

From *Christian Evidences and Ethics*

THEORIES OF CREATION

20. What is Theism, and has it any great defect in accounting for the Universe?

Theism claims the existence of one God, who not only has made the Universe, but who upholds and rules it. He is transcendent, that is, He is greater than the Universe He has made, and is independent of it. He is also immanent, that is, He is present in the Universe, upholding and ruling it. There does not seem to be any defect to this theory. It accounts for all the known facts in the Universe.

NOTE.—These theories are creations of our minds, the attempts we make to answer the question, how did the Universe come to exist? We know it exists. Our minds, in the constitution of their nature, must try to solve the mystery of its existence. We form these various theories during the history and experience of the race in the past and to-day. We are so far unable to form any other theories. We test all these theories by the knowledge we have of the Universe, a knowledge much wider and fuller to-day than has ever before been attained by mankind. Six of these theories do not stand the test; they should be discarded. One of the theories stands the test. The presumption is that it is true. But it is only a presumption. In such an important matter we cannot rest upon a presumption. Having eliminated the theories that do not satisfy, we must now ask for the theory that does satisfy, what are the evidences of its truth? Is it a theory only, or is it a reality? Is Theism a creation of the mind only, or is there a God as Theism has conceived there must be? In pursuing this study the grounds of Theism and the way in which it accounts for all the facts of the Universe must be concisely and carefully considered. The presumption in its favor will be sustained by various kinds of evidences, some more satisfactory to some minds than to others, but all having some force and the effect should be cumulative, turning the presumption into a certainty.

A diagram can be made bringing to the eye the results of these seven theories.

A circle represents the Universe. The unsatisfactory theories are represented by straight lines coming to the surface of the circle. The satisfactory theory is represented by a straight line going through the circle. This diagram may receive additions from the subject as we advance.

The unsatisfactory theories touch the surface, but do not go through the subject; they are superficial.

27. *What is the Evolutionary evidence of the existence of God?*

Evolution, as far as accepted by the various sciences, is a plan or law which man has discovered and described by which the various forces of nature have worked in all the past to bring about the present conditions, and by which they are now working to bring about future conditions. This plan implies One who formed it and who carries it out. Therefore, God exists.

NOTE.—This plan or law, the more wonderful it is seen to be, becomes a strong evidence of the existence of God, as He only could have formed it originally and have presided over its action through all the ages to bring about the present order. The plan discovered by our intelligence must have come from an intelligence not ourselves and far greater than ourselves. There is one great plan running through the Universe. Therefore, there is a God who formed and executes it. All things are evolved from prior things. Therefore, there is a God who is in nature or who originally endowed nature and has evolved it to its present condition.

28. *What is the plan of evolution, as man has been able to discover and describe it?*

Herbert Spencer, the leading evolutionary philosopher, formulates it as follows: "Evolution is an integration of matter and a concomitant dissipation of motion during which the matter passes from an indefinite incoherent homogeneity to a definite coherent heterogeneity, during which the retained motion undergoes a parallel transformation."

NOTE.—This far-famed description, made up of big unusual words, was builded up by Spencer from an examination of the many departments of the Universe covered by the various sciences of Astronomy, Geology, Biology, Zoölogy, Psychology and Sociology.

In the beginning, as described by Astronomy, the Universe was a widely extended cloud of gas or star dust. This gas was homogeneous, one kind, incoherent, not related, indefinite not separated, and in a swirl of motion.

Through the ages it shrank into a much smaller space. It integrated and some of the motion was dissipated, until now we have, as a part of it, our solar system; the sun and the planets are heterogeneous, of different kinds; they are coherent, related to each other; they are definite, separate and distinct from each other; and the retained motion has undergone a parallel transformation, the motion of our earth and its moon being its own, though related to that of the sun and the planets.

He traces this same transformation through all the sciences. We can note it now only in Sociology. The savage condition is homogeneous, men are alike; incoherent, not related; indefinite, not separated; a lot of men in a swirl of motion, eating, hunting, fishing, fighting. Our civilized nation is heterogeneous, men are of different kinds; coherent, related to each other; definite, separate and distinct from each other. The swirl of motion has been dissipated. The retained motion is that of order. There are farmers, manufacturers, merchants, the police, the army, the churches, the courts, the learned, the unlearned, dwelling together in an orderly organized society.

29. *How does evolution account for the various forms of life on the earth?*

It does not account for the introduction of life, only for its development. There is no evidence that life was evolved from dead matter. The highest organized crystal is different from the lowest living cell in that it is not living. The many forms of life were evolved from a single or a few simple forms. Life has the power of adapting itself to its surroundings. In doing this, it develops organs, and rudimentary organs become fully developed, as, e.g., a low form of life becomes sensitive to light; it has therein an additional power of adaptation; and this developing through many forms at last becomes a full organ, the eye itself.

30. *What are the limits of evolution?*

It never accounts for origins. It is a plan solely of development. At the beginning of Astronomy the homogeneous atoms were already existing. The present Universe has simply developed from them. At the beginning of Biology and Zoölogy life in lowest form was already existing, the many forms of life simply developed from it. Evolution does not claim to account for the original atom, or for the original life, either vegetable, animal or spiritual, only for its development.

31. *How does evolution, as far as known, become one of the strongest evidences of the existence of God?*

It is a great plan of development unifying all nature. But the plan does not account for itself. Man did not make it, he only discovered it. The atoms did not make it; they are its subjects. Life did not make it; it obeys it. God must have made it. Also, its limitations show the existence of God. It does not account for the wonderfully gifted atom, only for the development; nor for the wonderfully gifted germ of life, only for the development. God made the atom. God gave the life. God made the plan of development and presides over it.

NOTE.—It shows not only the existence of God, but also much of His wisdom and goodness. It is passing strange that Spencer, the great Agnostic, should have taught us so much of God. Taking the Universe as it exists to-day, coming from a vast succession of changes by the working of a simple plan, it is the realization of a great ideal or purpose. It is not yet complete, the plan is still going on. There is a further ideal or purpose.

The plan includes a multiplicity of details. Both wisdom and goodness are seen in that the plan makes progress necessary in all departments of nature, especially in life, both vegetable and animal. The far-famed expressions, "the struggle for existence" and the "survival of the fittest" show, when we take a wide, thoughtful view, a multiplicity of life forms in successive generations, ever rising in grades until man is reached. In the multitude of lower forms of quickly passing generations there is the largest conceivable amount of happiness, that of life. In the higher forms of life of slowly passing generations there is the largest conceivable quality of happiness, culminating in the intelligence of man.

32. *What is the Religious evidence of the existence of God?*

Man in his nature is a believer in God. He has in his nature an inherent sense of God and of his relation to him; he is in his nature a religious being. This is present, though low in degree, in the savage, the lowest man. It rises in degree with man's advance in civilization. It is not outgrown by any civilization yet attained. Man is adapted to believe in God as the eye is adapted to the light. Man's highest powers and noblest aspirations cannot be satisfied without God. Therefore, man concludes God exists. All nature shows supply of need, as, e.g., light to the eye. There is, therefore, God for the soul; or else there is a great lack, a vast exception in the highest reach of nature, which is . inconceivable.

Christian Evidences and Ethics.
Pages 16-17, 26-29.

From *The Sociology of the Bible*

Distribution of Wealth

The teachings of Christ about wealth are well worth a careful study by themselves, and should have special attention in these days of great riches. How large a proportion of His teachings were sociological as distinguished from and still closely related to theological is seen in many a chapter of his life. Take the tenth chapter of Mark's Gospel for example. He teaches about marriage, about children, about riches, about

His sacrifice upon the cross, about true greatness being the spirit of serving, and then He lays all His omnipotence at the feet of a blind beggar. The connection of the domestic relations and of the economic is not only in the chapter, but in the nature of the case. Restlessness in the marriage relation, dislike of children and the wrong view of wealth are closely related. It is quite evident the rich young man both in acquiring and in using riches loved them more than he loved his neighbor, his keeping of the second table of the law had been in letter more than in spirit. Christ loved him and pointed out to him his grave defect. He warned his disciples of this tendency of riches to lead to selfishness, and so shut out from the Kingdom of God, from the brotherhood of mankind. He showed them that love to God and love to one's neighbor would bring an abundance of riches and of friends. He tried to replace their self seeking with the spirit of service, the spirit of true greatness. Then he gave them His example both in teaching and in action.

There are four features of Christ's teaching about wealth, and his whole attitude toward it which can be easily traced and are in full harmony with the general teaching of the scriptures.

The first is its source. God is the giver of wealth, material prosperity comes from Him. God calls to account for the gaining and the using of wealth. God is the owner, man is the steward. Some of the parables giving pictures of wealth treat among other things of wealth itself. Man's varied talents are to be used in God's service. In gaining and using wealth man exercises his gifts as a servant of God, is acting with God. He as a steward must be always ready to give an account, must use his powers, and acquire and use wealth always in a way pleasing to God. The size of a modern fortune therefore does not count in Christ's sight, except as it answers the questions, did the millionaire gain his millions fairly as God's steward, and does he use his millions wisely in God's service.

The second feature is the law of acquirement. This is the law "love thy neighbor as thyself"; this is the Golden Rule. It applies to all hiring of labor, to all business transactions, to all enterprises great or small. The principle of love is not to be shut out of business, but is to control it. The accumulation of wealth goes hand in hand with the distribution of it. The great modern corporation is subject to the rule as well as the smallest individual with which it deals. It strives to secure only those dividends that are a fair equivalent for service rendered. A railroad corporation with the labor it hires and the general community it serves, is to love its employees and patrons as it loves its board of directors and its stockholders, and is to seek a mutual advantage for all as nearly equal as possible. This makes all business a matter of cooperation, a matter of fraternalism, it strives to be just and fair, to seek the good of others as it seeks its own. Adam Smith's rule "Let each individual and each nation seek for self, and a preestablished and divine order will make selfishness bring about the greatest good of the greatest number", overlooks the element of love in the highest stages of evolution. Christ's insight into "the preestablished and divine order" is finer and deeper. The love of self is to be kept within bounds for the "greatest good of the greatest number", by being made the standard of the love for others, then competition for self grows human by becoming competition for the service of others, and enthusiasm for self which is animal becomes enthusiasm for humanity which is social, and accumulation of wealth is secured in highest degree, together with its widest distribution. The competitive motive of Adam Smith does not bring about the greatest good of the greatest number—the social motive of Christ captures it and transforms it for the good of humanity.

The third feature of Christ's teaching about wealth is the comparative value of wealth and manhood. Christ never says anything against wealth itself, much of his teaching is in approval of the proper accumulation and distribution of wealth, but he never for an instant loses sight of the fact that a man is worth more than a sheep. He is never confused as to the relativity of values. A fortune, however great, the whole world itself, is as nothing when compared with man. Adam Smith's political economy makes wealth the center, and man revolves around it. Christ's political economy makes man the center, and wealth revolves around him. Like the ptolemaic theory of the solar system Adam Smith is mistaken; he is behind the times; and is being set aside. Like the Copernican theory, Christ is correct, and is being more widely adopted, and holds the future in His grasp. Manhood is the supreme product of the institution of industry. The policy of any society should be the production of manhood. The accumulation and distribution of wealth is not the end in view, it is only a means to the end, the end is manhood. Man is worth more than a railroad, a coal mine or a bank vault, he is worth more than a palace or a church, he is worth more than a painting or a poem. Christ would ask of a modern factory not how much money does it make but how much manhood, of modern civilization not how rich it is, but what kind of men and women does it have. Christ's teaching will not allow us to consider wealth as an aim. Business for profit only is essentially immoral. Wealth must not be considered by itself but as a part of a great whole, it must be in harmony, for instance, with psychology, man's mental powers, and with ethics, man's moral nature, it must be in harmony with government and religion. Manhood produces wealth, but wealth does not produce manhood. Honesty, industry, skill, self-control, obedience to law, willingness and ability to co-operate are the sources of wealth; these create wealth. Deceit, trickery, fraud, self-seeking do not create wealth; they rob and destroy. Christ's teachings of wealth are a part of a complete whole, they cover the fulness and harmony of man's powers in the Kingdom of God. It is misleading to enumerate land, labor and capital as the factors of wealth production, the formula should include mental and moral character, the fully rounded manhood of Christ's Kingdom. Let barbarians have all the capital and land, all the mines and farms, all the factories and railroads of our civilization, and let them labor with all their might and they would produce not wealth but ruin. They would seek to enjoy, not to serve. A wonderful amount of the spirit of service has sway in Christian civilization, it is only where man has learned to serve his brother man that it is at all safe for him to hold the great forces of nature in his grasp.

There may be some civil war in the social science of Christian lands today, but political economy is the rebel against the rights of man, not Christ. Government may say, Democracy, the power is in the people. Political Economy may say Aristocracy, the power is in the few. Jurisprudence may say, Justice is the equality of rights, the law of love, the law of service. Political economy may say, Self interest is the law, the conquest by the few in competition with the many. Christ is evidently on the side of the Government, and of Jurisprudence. Manhood is the supreme product of a wise social science, it is the final object of all laws and policies, including all political and industrial institutions; and wealth in its accumulation and distribution is of value only as a means to this end. Christian industrialism produces and distributes wealth without wasting more than it produces or destroying values higher than it creates, it makes manhood the ultimate object of thought and labor. It is far better for the Christian pulpit to preach and for the Christian church to live according to the Golden Rule of Christ, than according to the Political Economy of Adam Smith.

The fourth feature of Christ's teaching about wealth is found in his uniform conduct to the wealthy men of His day, and to the poor. The Pharisees were, as a rule, a wealthy class. Christ never criticised them for their wealth in itself, though he was very severe against such as in gaining wealth had devoured widows houses, or had forgotten judgment mercy and faith in their business dealings, or those that made a show of their wealth in building monuments. He went freely to the homes of the rich, socially and on missions of love, he feasted with them, taught them and healed their sick, he comforted them in their sorrow and rejoiced with them in their joys. He selected some of his disciples from the wealthy class. Capernaum is called his city. He selected it as the

center of His activity when in Galilee, it was a wealthy city whose
marble palaces were reflected in the waters of the beautiful lake, and
whose marts were frequented by the merchants of many lands; He
chose it as His home rather than the wilds of Gadara. Some of his closest
friends were wealthy. He loved Mary and Martha and Lazarus who
were rich, and their home of luxury at Bethany was always his home
when He visited Jerusalem; in the seclusion of its richness and love He
spent the day of silence in passion week, and from it he passed with
His disciples to the upper room of some wealthy friend in Jerusalem;
and then on alone to the cross.

While he had relations of helpfulness and friendship with the rich he
treated the poor with equal kindness. He went to the houses of the
poor as freely as to those of the rich. He gave His gracious ministries
to the poor as lovingly as to the rich, his teachings were as full and frank
with the poor as to the rich. It was suffering humanity that appealed to
Him, and He cured the poor as freely as the rich. You cannot tell simply
from His action or from His speech whether He is associating with the
rich or the poor, with master or laborer, mistress or maid. He made no
distinction between the rich and the poor. He treated all alike. He
attached no moral quality to the condition of either the rich or the poor.
He was always attentive to the needs of manhood. That His conduct
was such a contrast to that of other teachers may account for His reply
to John the Baptist, bewildered and cast down in prison, but it is more
probable that the nature of his message and the special attention He
gave to the more needy are involved in it. At any rate His answer to
John was that one of the evidences that He was the Messiah was that
He preached the Gospel to the poor, the good tidings of the Kingdom
of God to the poor.

It is quite evident that if the Church is anything like her Lord there
will be little cause of calling her a partisan of either the rich or the poor.
She will seek to minister equally to both, she will cordially welcome in
her membership both, the one as cordially as the other, she will try in
both cases, equally, to cultivate the true manhood in Christ. Still there
is something of a kindred condition existing today as in Christ's time,
and if she is challenged by any of the bewildered and oppressed she
aught to be able to reply as Christ replied, "The Gospel is preached to
the poor", freely, lovingly as Christ preached it. The apostles carried
on the teachings of Christ concerning the supreme values of manhood
and the fraternal spirit in business and the accumulating and distribution
of wealth. The early disciples in Jerusalem tried the experiment of voluntary holding of wealth as a common possession in their own little
circle. The quickly arising case of Ananias and Sapphira taught them

the supreme value of truth in individual and social character, the worth of manhood, and that their holding wealth in common was of secondary importance. On the other hand there arose the spirit of giving special honor and privilege to the rich in the little circle of the disciples, and this was sternly rebuked by James to the Jewish Christians and by Paul to the Corinthians. The spirit of fraternalism found unchecked and wisely directed exercise in the loving care of the poor in each little circle of disciples, and in the sympathy and help of one section to another though widely separated in space and in race, so the world was amazed and said, "How Christians love each other".

When we consider the great accumulation of wealth in modern time in Christian lands, especially in our land, we see at a glance that there is much of the spirit of fraternalism in it. It is astonishing that so much has been accumulated in a century or two as to give ground for the opinion that the world is now at least twice as wealthy as it was two centuries ago, from the results of man's gaining dominion over the earth in all the former centuries. This modern wealth as distinguished from the former wealth of the world arises almost entirely from two things, discovery and invention. The main discoveries have been of coal, petroleum, the expansive powers of steam and the positive and negative properties of electricity. The inventions have been of mechanical contrivances for utilizing these great discoveries in the service of mankind. It is with discovery as with invention, both are for the race. He who discovered the expansive power of steam discovered it not for himself but for the race. He who invented the steam engine invented it not for himself but for the race. The laws of society give the discoverer and the inventor some reward, but at best it can be but a very small share in the results of a great service of mankind.

So the wealth of today while the greater part is still in land values, differs in kind also from the wealth of past centuries. That was largely in houses, in garments, in the precious metals and in jewels. These have not lost any of their value, through all the changing centuries jewels are still sought and cherished. But all these things that may be grasped and used by the few are but a very small part of the wealth of the world today. Today's wealth is largely in railroad and steamships, in telegraphs and telephones, in things that are of use to all, and virtually belong to mankind. While not quite as free as the air, they are about as common as the air, they may be used by all the people at small charge, and some of the greatest at no charge at all, they are virtually owned by all the people. The railroad magnate may ride in his private car; but it is generally concluded that the ordinary cars are more comfortable, and a ride in them is more entertaining. The palace on the avenue may be ablaze with light and the robes and jewels vie with oriental splendor, but the lights on the street are also bright and the crowds there are better clothed than the wealthy of former centuries, and far out in the dark country there is a room more cozy and a light better to read by than the palace can afford. The vast accumulation of wealth is in its nature far more widely distributed than of yore, and than is generally recognized.

Still no one can fail to see that there are shadows, and some of them very black ones, that there is a spirit abroad different from the spirit of service, that Adam Smith has followers as well as Jesus Christ. There is great cause for the terms so prevalent today, swollen fortunes, predatory wealth, ostentatious riches, while there is also abundant cause for the term beneficient fortunes, serving wealth and adorning riches. The wealth of the United States in 1850 was seven billions of dollars, in 1900 it was ninety-four billions of dollars, an immense accumulation. Nearly one-half the wealth is in land values, and much of this has made its great increment by the means of railroads. The ownership of the farm lands is still widely distributed, though a marked tendency prevails toward large estates.

But concerning the general distribution of the vast accumulation of wealth in our country some startling statements are made by careful students. It is claimed by these careful students that one per cent of the families of the United States own over one-half of the whole great wealth, one-half the ninety-four billions of dollars; and that less than ten per cent of the families own over three-quarters of the ninety-four billions of dollars. On the other hand these students say that ten per cent of the people of these wealthy United States are in poverty. They support themselves with great difficulty and at the best cannot maintain their lives in healthy efficiency, they are underfed, underclothed and underhoused, and are constantly affording many recruits to the ranks of pauperism, to be supported at the public expense. It is said the average income of the average family of five in the United States, is less than seven hundred dollars a year. That surely is not far removed from poverty, it is on the verge of it; except of course in minister's families where high thinking makes them skillful in plain living. The unskilled laborer earns less than four hundred and fifty dollars a year in the north, and less than three hundred dollars in the south; that is the average laborer can support a family only in poverty, he must be helped by women and young children. Many wage earners certainly can live only from hand to mouth; they must necessarily do so, if, as Adam Smith's followers say, the price of labor is measured by the lowest cost of living. To solve the problem of living not only must the income be considered but the outgo, and bare subsistence is certainly not the ideal in the Kingdom of God; even in that stage of it already reached in a Christian land. Dr. Devine, Secretary of the Charity Organization of New York City, says that for a family of five persons the minimum income to maintain "any approach to a decent standard of living is $600. a year." Prof. Small of the University of Chicago says "no man can bring up a family and enjoy ordinary human happiness on a wage of less than $1000. a year". John Mitchell estimates the minimum wages that will maintain a working man and his family "in the coal regions according to the American standard" at $600. a year. Many prominent social workers in New York and Chicago agree that $900. was the minimum wages to support a family of five in decency. The Maryland Bureau of Statistics puts the minimum amount at $750. a year and places the figures as follows. House rent $180., Market and groceries $364., Clothing $85., Insurance $18. Amusements, papers, books and incidentals $10. Doctor and medicine $20. Coal and light $35., carfare, as only such low house rent can be obtained in the suburbs of Baltimore, $30. If the average income of a family of five in the United States is less than $700. a year, there must be many families below the average, below the power of decent living. The cost of living is variable in different sections and in different times. The United States Bureau of Labor shows the relation of the cost of living to average annual incomes in the year 1905 as compared with the ten years period 1890 and 1900; the cost of living in 1905 was 16 per cent higher than the average for the ten year period, while the wage earnings in 1905 were only 14 per cent higher than the average for the ten year period. This shows that Christ's standard of wages "Love thy neighbor as thyself", that is, what is he worth to me, has not gained but rather lost a little in the last fifteen years, if such general statistics have only one cause, which of course is improbable; but these fifteen years have been years of great prosperity and the showing ought to have been on the other side, making due allowance for all conceivable causes.

By the census of 1900 there were more than 18,000,000 wage earners in the United States, not salaried men nor business men, nor professional men nor proprietors but those employed and paid wages; as these of course are mostly adults, and a large majority men, they form a large proportion of our population which in that year was 76,000,000. The wage problem is certainly worthy of thoughtful consideration of all lovers of mankind. The size of the problem comes largely from the largeness of modern enterprises. They cannot be divided up among a great number of small proprietors each doing largely for himself and family, and having few employees, they must be carried on by a few directors with a vast number of wage earners.

The Sociology of the Bible.
Pages 254-263.

VIII
Graham Taylor, 1851-1938

Graduating in 1851, Graham Taylor, after a Reformed Church pastorate, served as professor at both Hartford and Chicago Congregational Seminaries. A pioneer in the new fields of Christian social work and thought that were developing in the latter nineteenth century, he was founder of a well known social settlement, the Chicago Commons. The quotation is from *Religion in Social Action* (1913), and expresses ideas similar to those of his contemporary, Ferdinand Schenck, then teaching at New Brunswick.

Industry and Religion

The present crisis in industrial relationship tests the capacity of the Christianity of the churches to adapt itself to the modern conditions of life, and marks the point at which it will either make another great advance or suffer a sharp decline. It must find terms of economic and industrial relationship in which to express and impress its sanctions, if it is to survive, much more guide and dominate life in this industrial age. And our system and methods of industry must find terms of religious spirit and fellowship in which to justify their claim to be forces making for righteousness and for the progress of the race. This interdependence of religion and industry states the problem of finding common ground, on which they make it possible for each other to fulfil their essential function, a common ground upon which religious industrial life may become actual in this age of the world.

There are at least three human interests upon which both industry and religion set their value. At three points the industrial and religious valuations must either find a common denominator or be fatally exclusive of each other. Religion and industry test each other by the valuation which each puts upon every human life, upon the standard of living, upon union through sacrifice as essential to progress.

Upon each human life religion has ever placed a divine valuation. In both the Jewish and Christian faiths God identifies himself with each single self, by creating man in his own image and likeness and by standing in between each life and self-neglect or the aggression of others. When the king of Israel was self-convicted of blood-guiltiness in sending a common soldier to his death, he cried out, as though he had struck at the very life of God, "Against thee, thee only, have I sinned." The Roman who was capable of coining the sentiment "Nothing that is common to man is foreign to me," was also capable of divorcing his wife because she did not expose to death the girl-baby born in his absence, so disappointed was he that the child was not a boy. Yet at that very time Christianity began to invest every life with such a divine sanctity that the law of every Christian nation has ever since gotten in between, not only the parent and the child, but between even the mother and the unborn babe. In America we put a valuation upon every child so great that we can afford to make the school tax heavy rather than to have any boy or girl grow up uneducated. The right to life is so sacred

85

that every community in Christendom bears the burden of providing food, clothing, and shelter to every helpless person, no matter how useless to self or others such an one may be. More than by any speech, symbol, or act of man, "the cross" sets God's estimate upon the value of every man, woman, and child. And it has imposed upon the religious conscience that sense of the worth of a life which is expressed in what we call "the burden of the soul."

How then does the industrial valuation of the same life accord with the religious value of the soul? Our economists, indeed, estimate each able-bodied working-man's life to be worth at least two thousand dollars to the working wealth of the nation. But in shameless inconsistency with these estimates of our religious, ideal, and economic valuation stands the industrial depreciation of the value of a human life. Let the price-mark on a life be set by the overwork of women, with which the courts are interfering to protect the nation and the race from the deterioration of their offspring. Let the insatiable waste of child labour be measured by the instinct of self-protection which forces nations to protect themselves from the industrial depletion of the very stock of the race. Let the frightful industrial casualties in America sound the depths of our own disregard of human life and safety by the lists of the dead and wounded, disabled and missing, which in some industries exceed the casualties of the deadliest battle-fields of our worst wars. Let our conscienceless indifference to the grievous burden imposed by the bread-winner's death be arraigned by our prolonged refusal to distribute that burden of supporting the dependent families of the slain or disabled workers as it is distributed in other lands between the owners of the industry, the taxpayers of the state, and the wage-earners.

What makes the workaday life a tragedy is the hopelessly inconsistent disparity between the valuation which the industries and the religion of the same people put upon the same life. The claim of religious people to love the "soul," seems the cruelest hypocrisy when identified with the heedless carelessness for the very life of the same person. It would seem that to make good its claims to bearing the burden of souls, religion must find concrete measures of industrial protection in which to express its care for the lives of men. And yet, until very recently, the working people of America have been left alone by the influential constituencies of the churches to make their hard and heroic struggle for self-protection. First in the field, hardest at work has organised labour been to protect the religious and educational sanctity of each working life, to regulate or suppress child labour, to shorten the hours and improve the conditions of women's work.

But efforts of others should not be forgotten. The splendid initiative

of the Earl of Shaftesbury in placing the factory acts on the statute books
of England two generations ago has led men and women from all classes
ever since, and never more than now, to unite to protect and enhance
the value of life. More and more the forces of religion and civilisation
are uniting in such concerted movements as the National Child Labour
Committee, the Consumers' League, the Visiting Nurses' Association,
and many other voluntary agencies to co-operate with factory inspectors,
truant officers, and juvenile courts in the enforcement of just and hu-
mane legislation. Thus the sanctions of religion and education upon the
value of a life are being translated in terms, economic and industrial,
by every protected piece of machinery which keeps the fingers on the
hand and the hand on the arm; by all the hygienic and sanitary conditions provided for in shops; by all the efforts for industrial insurance; by
all the life-saving appliances and conditions on the waterways and the
railways of the land; and wherever safety is in peril in the working
world.

The standard of living affords another common ground on which religion and industry are found to be interdependent. In raising the standard of living to be compatible with the value of life, both industry
and religion realise their ideal. By holding over every one's head the
ideal of what a human life was meant and made to be, religion lifts the
standards of that life, creates a divine discontent with anything less and
lower, and stirs men to struggle singly and together to maintain and
advance a rising scale of living which comes to be as dear as life itself.
The response of industry to this ideal of religion is the demand for the
opportunity to earn such a livelihood as will make the realisation of that
idea possible. The struggle of working people to raise and maintain their
standard of living is due to the best that is in them and not to the worst.
"If this is the kind of a man or woman religion and education teach me
to be," the worker naturally concludes, "I should be given the chance
to earn the living of such a man or woman." Interpreted in human terms
"the standard of living" means the rest which the son of a working
mother thinks she should have in her old age, the exemption which his
wife should have from wage-earning in order to mother his children,
the schooling his boy or girl should get before going out into the working
world. The rising standards of living are due to the ideal which religion
has taught us all to have of manhood and womanhood, fatherhood and
motherhood, wifehood and childhood.

Employers who have too long and too widely united to hold down
and retard the rise in labour's standard of living, have more and more
to their credit many and varied unselfish efforts and achievements in
lifting the standards of labour's livelihood and opening to ever-increasing

multitudes the opportunity and means of realising it. Both among employers and employés the struggle to achieve the rising standard of living for the class and the mass should be sanctified by religion. It should be no small part of our personal and collective religious aim and effort not only to protect our fellow men from lowering the standard of their living by establishing a minimum wage, but also to help them raise it, and keep it rising, above a mere living wage, as far as the conditions of the trade or craft will allow. Until we thus translate our religious love of souls into our economic care for selves, religion will mean very little to those who are in the struggle for life and livelihood in an industrial age.

A third common ground on which religion and industry are seen to be interdependent is defined by the fact that both have taught men to sacrifice in order to unite for the common good. Have we not been teaching, drilling, disciplining our men, women, and children—at home, at school, and at church; by their loyalty to family, party, patriotism, and faith—to sacrifice self and stand together for the common good of all or any of them? Have we not invested with patriotic and even religious sanctity those who sacrifice themselves for "their own" folk, fatherland, or faith? How then do these virtues suddenly become vices, these heroes and heroines all at once become sordid conspirators when they combine, stake everything dear to each, risk all, and stop short of the loss of nothing, in united action to save their own or their fellow workers' standard of living? They may do so in unwise or even unjust ways, but we submit that what is by common consent considered wholly meritorious in every other sphere for self-sacrifice cannot be wholly reprehensible in that of industrial relationship where it is hardest and costliest to exercise the virtues of altruism. What is attributed to the very best in men elsewhere cannot be attributed to the very worst in men here. The "union" of labourers cannot differ, *per se*, morally and as an economic necessity from a combination of capitalists or the communion of members of the same religious faith. If, at this age of the world, combination is necessary to success, where is the justice in forcing these competitors of ours to do their business with us as though they lived in that former age of the world when each one could mind his own business without combining with others?

It looks then as though the industrial world has outgrown our moral sense, as though our ethics are hopelessly belated, for we seem to want to make our profits under the modern method of combining all available resources, while at the same time insisting that our fellow workers shall deal with us under the old outworn and discarded system of individual industry. That is, we want others to do unto us as we are not willing to do unto them. It looks as though some of us were being tried and found wanting. Of "times that try men's souls" we speak as though they were to be dreaded and yet belong to the "heroic age," but when we look back upon them from safe distance, we are generally forced to confess that the "times" were not more out of joint than that the "souls"—our own or others'—needed to be tried.

Religion in Social Action.
Pages 177-189.

IX
Edward Strong Worcester, 1876-1937

Dr. Worcester came to New Brunswick as professor of theology from a Congregationalist pastorate, with theological education at Hartford and Berlin. From the beginning, he was a center of controversy over charges of heterodoxy that rested on misunderstandings, and on the sharp division caused by the fundamentalist-modernist controversy. These limited his influence in the denomination, but the qualities of deep devotion, scholarly attainment, and unflinching honesty, reflected in his inaugural address of 1924, here reprinted, made a lasting impression on those who knew him.

The Parish Minister and His Theology

Were I to consult simply my own sense of the proprieties on this occasion, I should be more than content to make humble acknowledgment of the inspiring ardor and sound wisdom with which sermon and charge have laid upon my conscience some part in the opportunity which lies before the church today, and so leave the matter. The pastor at installation is assigned a listening part, and the teacher just entering upon new lines of duty can hardly be looked to for the wisdom that is to come, as he hopes, with more experience. He has plans, to be sure, ideals, methods he longs to put to trial, else he might well infer that he had no call to the teaching office; but he holds them subject to enlightenment and the test of practice. Christian theology in particular is a profound and complex discipline, even as the faith with which it deals is far-reaching and glorious. I am not minded jauntily to adventure a program of teaching method—nor would one half-hour suffice for the telling of all there is in the gospel of the Son of God that seems to me worthy of apprehension and presentation with every power of the most ardent soul.

On the other hand, it is hardly necessary for me here, as in some other positions it might be, to make detailed confession of my faith or elaborate its relation to the historic developments of Christianity. Something of this was before the General Synod a year ago—in ways not altogether of my choosing but no doubt sufficient for the purpose!

Let me rather, then, as one newly come from the varied concerns of the pastorate, and hopeful that whatever studies I have opportunity to share with young men looking forward to like occupations may serve to prepare them for a more inspiring and adequate ministry as ambassadors of the Lord Christ, speak for a little of the parish minister as theologian. For I am well convinced that he cannot afford not to be one, if he is to rise at all to the largeness of his responsibility, and equally certain that by bringing to his theology perverted aims or an unworthy temper he can readily qualify in the company of those for whom, since they cause the Master's little ones to stumble, it were better that a millstone should be hanged about their neck, and that they should be cast into the sea.

The demand so often made for a distinction between theology and religion—I noticed it again in a book advertisement only the other day—is an entirely proper demand. I grant that these two words cannot mean the same to any intelligent person. I cheerfully admit that the possession of theological opinions, however correct, is no guarantee that the possessor is in the active enjoyment of a religious life. The reverse contention, also somewhat vocal, that the religious life can and should, in the experience of those who are truly spiritual and intelligent, be innocent of all theology, I am not so ready to admit. "Man is a being," says Prof. Sterrett, "who thinks all his experience, and perforce must think his religious experience." And while it is evident that a considerable number of men and women go through a variety of experiences of moment, religious and other, without troubling to interpret or relate them, or to think about them in any clear and orderly way at all, I see no reason why that bland unconcern should be held up as a model— unless, indeed, we are to take the position that faith is hardly faith when one knows what it is and has reasons for it.

For the minister such unconcern is well-nigh impossible. Week by week he is called upon to open the Scriptures. He proclaims the gospel of Christ. He labors for His kingdom. Besides the need of depth and vitality in his own inner being, he deals with the spiritual needs of others in endless variety; his charge is a "cure of souls." How can he do all this without understanding, or understand without thought?

At the Life Work Conference so successfully held at this seminary a few weeks ago one of our pastors named what he considered the three chief functions of the ministry. One of these had to do with social relations and the removal of class suspicion and misunderstanding. The other two—let me cite them as I took them down at the time: To interpret life in terms of the spirit; to answer the questions people ask about the religious life. Do you tell me that the average pastor, especially in the turmoil of a modern industrial city, has other things to concern him than theology, other matters more needful to think about? I beg to refer you to a testimony like this—and it is not isolated—as it came out of a busy pastor's experience, not at a symposium of scholars, but in an appeal to boys and young men to consider the largeness of the minister's opportunity. Two points out of three are theology, and nothing less, explain it how you will.

For theology, strange to say, is not a mass of metaphysical speculation or abstruse dogmatism, incomprehensible thoughts laid out (*absit omen!*) in incomprehensible terms. It is just the thinking out and setting forth in some orderly fashion of the facts and grounds and hopes of the religious life. As long as there are living souls in our parishes there will be questions as to how we or the world came to be, and to what it is all tending, and how we know that God is, and what manner of being He is, and what proof we have that in His infinite preoccupations He notices us or cares, and, if He cares, what His will is for us, and how eyes blinded by sin are to see Him, and how hearts enamored of self are to turn to Him, and why the Bible is as unescapable as conscience, and the meaning of the wonder of Christ, and the secret of the power of His cross, and the scope of the promise of His kingdom, and what lies on the farther side of death, and I know not how much besides.

There is more theology in this world than its detractors dream of. The old lady of story who found that she had been talking prose all her life and never knew it has her counterpart in many an earnest and wistful spirit who seeks an answer to theological inquiries without suspecting that they are theology. Now the fact that one can speak in prose without knowing the name is no reason why he need do so. Those especially who are called on to make a lifetime's use of persuasive speech will be no worse for realizing what prose is and inquiring into its laws and possibilities, its rhythm, and its structure. So too those who are to specialize in religion, who aspire to be leaders in religious endeavor and are called upon to guide the spiritual experience of many, may not blithely dispense with thought upon the subject, serious thought, consecutive thought, illuminating reflection.

In a recent reading of the life of Augustus St. Gaudens I was struck again with the emphasis which the master in sculpture puts upon the study of anatomy. It is probable that he has no intention at all of modelling a skeleton for exhibition, and quite possible that only a small part of his finished work will show the undraped figure. And yet what hours of concentration he devotes to ascertaining the body's inner structure, the action of the muscles upon the frame, and all their varying interplay. Why not simply "draw the thing as he sees it"—the outward thing that everybody sees, and is to see again in the artist's reproduction? For the great figure of the standing Lincoln, for example, why is not the hang of the coat and the poise of head and hands enough? Because he is drawing not alone for the passing observer, but "for the God of things as they are," and because—mark this—because he does not know the thing he sees until he knows it as it is.

I contend, then, that the preacher of righteousness and the herald of the gospel of redemption is not adequately or surely prepared for the simplest tasks of Christian preaching and pastoral guidance unless he knows something more than the surface effects with which he is dealing—unless he knows what righteousness *is*, in its roots and its structure and its animating power, unless he knows what his gospel *is*, and the meaning and source and goal of the redemption he proclaims. The physician who should solemnly look at my tongue with no perception at all of the facts that lie deeper than the surface of it would be no more of a charlatan than the pastor who undertakes to deal with the unfortunate symptoms of a disordered life but spares himself the labor of grappling with the significance of either sin or salvation. The pulpit from which moral platitudes are megaphoned, or even familiar phrases about new birth, trust in a Saviour's sacrifice, eternal death and life, whose actual meaning the preacher could not explain in any other words to save his soul, is after all not so much better than a Chinese prayer-wheel.

God's herald needs to know the God that sent him. Christ's envoy ought to understand both who Christ is and what is His thought concerning us. How shall he lead the people where he himself has hardly begun to follow? How shall he feed the flock from an empty store? Is it not the first and great commandment that a man shall love God with all his heart and soul and mind? Truly, "the heart does make the theologian"; it gives the color and the life to his endeavor. But "we have the mind of Christ" is also good doctrine. And a mindless minister is almost as sad a sight as a heartless one.

You will have guessed, perhaps, that I do not consider the pursuit of this life-giving knowledge a purely intellectual process. Pascal is still right in saying, "The heart hath its reasons which the reason doth not know." St. Paul is still right in saying that "the things of the spirit are spiritually discerned." Jesus Christ is still right in saying, "He that willeth to do shall know." In other words, it takes the whole of a man—and the grace of God besides—to apprehend the gospel and interpret it. That is one of the terrifying things about the ministry. It is also one of the things that make it the incomparable calling.

There are some theological moods which can be dispensed with, I think, both in the seminary and in the parish. In others theology is as much needed as it ever was, or more. May I try to indicate which?

For one, I doubt if the Christian pastor and teacher need greatly concern himself with a theology that is apologetic either in the popular or in the technical sense. Apologetics is often defined as Christianity defensively stated. But why state it defensively? I cannot feel that Christian truth much needs our defending. It needs to be proclaimed, and proclaimed much more fairly and intelligibly. It needs to be lived, and lived much more consistently and persuasively. When that is done it will commend itself, with no great need of apology.

On the theological side what is essential for proof is already involved in statement and exposition, if the statement is fair and the exposition adequate. On the practical side the tree is known by its fruits, and no amount of discourse will make amends for the lack of them, just as no amount of contrary argument can undo a fact or counterbalance the persuasive force of a life. On the philosophical side we are a long way from those early days when Christianity was a novelty and apologetics arose in the works of the great apologists. Instead of presenting a newcomer's claim to be heard among a goodly company of established philosophies, we are laying our own metaphysical foundations and connecting the Christian view with the scheme of things in general, not defensively, but constructively. In those seminaries which have two or more chairs in the department of theology you will have noticed, perhaps, that in the division of functions between apologetics, dogmatics, and ethics, the first item has become in fact chiefly philosophy of religion.

There are doubts for the Christian pastor to deal with which are philosophic in their origin. My point is that they must be forestalled with a sounder philosophy, and that his attitude must be positive, not negative. The church commits a major error today if it allows itself to be put on the defensive by (for example) materialism. The Christian faith has been in the world a long time now, and theism longer still. Its world-view is most comprehensive, it goes to the roots of things, it faces ultimate problems as courageously as any. Its interpretation of life has met the tests of time and use. Its fruits in practice, though confessedly immature and far short as yet of its exacting ideal, are gratifying and abundant. Measured not merely by the number of its adherents but— what is far more important—by the quality of its chief souls and the spiritual power of those who have held it truth, Christianity is no contemptible theory. I decline to put it on the defensive. If there is going to be any fighting, let us carry the war into Africa and make the materialist show cause why his view has any claim upon our faith.

On the historical side—since Christianity has its roots in history—it will always be possible to raise questions concerning this or that record or evidence of its origin. For these the minister's training in New Testament history and criticism will prepare him, rather than his theology. But here, too, the defensive is not his best position. When doubts arise as to the actuality of a supposed historical occurrence, he should not be content with the negative argument that there is no sufficient reason why we may not believe it, but address himself also to the reasons why we should.

On the Scriptural side I doubt if our valiant "defenses" have bettered matters. The Bible has suffered more in common esteem from the extravagances of its apologists than from the assaults of its enemies. The oak in the forest does not need my anxious shielding from winter's blasts. The sword does not ask defending in the sheath. The Word of God is no weakling; it will give an excellent account of itself if we give it free play.

Why not have done with all this dreary "repelling of assaults," and "meeting of criticism," and head-wagging over the prevalence of doubt, and plugging holes in the dike with desperate fingers? Suppose we forget all that, and preach our gospel in the fullness of it and live our life like loyal men of God. A church which persists in fighting rear-guard actions and falling back from one untenable entrenchment to another is bound to be miserable. Let it take the field to which its Captain leads. His promise was not that from behind the walls of some last citadel we should hold the forces of iniquity at bay, but that the gates of death on the defensive should not be able to prevail.

It may be that these martial figures will suggest that I am disposed to revive the ancient title of my chair, which denominated its theology as polemic. If so, let me hasten to assure you that I have never taken "Fight the good fight of faith" as the setting forth of a controversial ideal. A sinner converted is better than ninety-and-nine controverted; and controversy among saints is civil war. It is a curious fact that when theologians have confronted unbelief without they have developed what they call apologetics, but when they have dealt with one another in the inevitable differences of interpretation of God's wealth of truth the result has been even more aptly termed polemics. A fighting mood, a militant Christianity, is all very well in its place. But its place is not among fellow-Christians, who trust in the one Saviour and Lord and are honestly trying to discern His will. Moreover our warfare should be more a moral than an intellectual exercise. Against selfishness and unclean-ness, against oppression and strife, against vice and dishonor, against spiritual hosts of wickedness in high places, and against their own cherished sins, let Christians go forth, not treading softly, as so often, but terrible as an army with banners. That would be a polemic worth furthering.

Alas! as a matter of fact it has been quite other, and the result we know. There are few spectacles over which evil in morals and falsehood in thought can better afford to chuckle than that of faith's exponents busied with mutual annihilation anent divine decrees, or Joshua's astronomy, or the date of the end of the world. Theologians who make it their chief business to bite and devour one another are so nearly consumed of one another that they occasion the common enemy little concern. Shepherds of Jesus' flock are ill occupied in stirring up the sheep to combat. Guides are in truth no guides, whose idea of leading in the way of life is endless denunciation of the paths that others seem to their hasty temper to be following. Think of fitting out men who are to be Christ's ministers in this eager day with nothing better than a syllabus of errors and a bagful of refutations! Think of pastors and preachers with nothing more vital to impart than an identification of the flaws in others' teaching! That such may be able to stir up hot enthusiasm for a time I do not doubt. Most men have an imp in them somewhere which is happy at Donnybrook Fair, where the one rule of the game is "If you see a head, hit it!" But for all that I maintain that the theology of the parish minister should not be controversial. "The Lord's servant must not strive."

On the contrary, if he wants to be of true service in this time of much mingling of peoples and confusion of ideas, let him aspire to be comprehensive. It is not only a matter of grave doubt whether any one of us has an infallible grasp of all the truth of God, but it is a question worthy of consideration whether any man who trusts Christ and earnestly follows Him can be wholly given over to lies. Will it never occur to us that, with all the apparent distortion, omission, or extravagance that separates his view from ours, this other may have some light of living truth that we have missed? Is it better to learn from him where he is right, or send him to the stake for what he has got wrong?

This comprehension may well be historical as well as contemporary. I believe it was Col. Higginson who said that no man could properly call himself a liberal until he knew better than to kick his grandfather's opinions downstairs. Childhood accepts the parental or grandparental view with little question. Youth in the reaction of its new-found selfhood is quite likely to reject it with as little discrimination. It belongs to a maturity which some of us never quite reach to make just appraisals, and, unencumbered with futile luggage of antiquities or novelties, set forth the abundant treasure of things new and old, things that are cherished not for their party label or their date, but for their worth.

How then does it fare with the theology that is dogmatic? In the original, etymological sense, the minister—or layman, for that matter— might properly enough aspire to be just that, for dogma meant first a belief or opinion, and then such opinion definitely formulated. Formulation with due regard for all the factors is a wholesome exercise for any thinker. Dr. Hartranft, who was so well known here before he went to New England to guide and inspire a generation of theologues, used to advise us to write out a fresh creed once a year for the sake of clarity and comprehension. But that is the individual pursuit of truth—the faith which one has to oneself before God, as the apostle puts it. And we all know, alas! that "dogma," "dogmatic," and "dogmatism" have come with the passage of time to be horses of quite another color. It is not for theologians to complain, for if the modern world has accepted the words as synonyms for all that is dictatorial and unreasoning, who but the theologians made them so? It is rather for us to bring forth fruits

worthy of repentance, to show that it is possible to be clear without
being arrogant, to have convictions without closing one's mind, to have
reasons and trust to their very reasonableness to persuade without dom-
ineering or dragooning or intimidating.

Any pastor who has lent a sympathetic ear to the wide-ranging questions of his high-school boys knows that he needs a mind alert, well
trained, and humble if he is to answer them. Crushing assertions will
not do. The steam-roller does not make good Christians. The compilers
of the Athanasian Creed spoiled what might have been a useful piece
of work when they framed it in damnatory clauses. I do not know much
about the psychology of their time, but no young man of spirit today is
disposed to "willing acceptance" of opinions shot at him in that fashion.
Damnatory dogmatism damns itself first of all. It is unnecessary, to
begin with, it is provocative, it is un-Christ-like—though it is perpet-
uated to this hour by many earnest and well-meaning persons, and
applied to a great many other subjects than the Trinity.

Systematic is a better term than any that preceded it in this department. In so far as it calls for orderly rather than haphazard procedure
and implies an effort to interpret the facts of religion in their organic
unity, relating part harmoniously with part, rather than flinging together
a medley of disjointed observations, it reflects a worthy ideal not only
for the class-room but for the pastor's study. The danger which must be
guarded against is simply that which attaches to all "systems"—filing
systems, for a familiar example—namely, that system may become an
obsession and a tyrant, vault into the saddle and ride the poor system-
atizer to a fall. It is the temptation to fit everything in, whether we
have mastered the situation sufficiently to perceive how it fits or must
complete our task by the method of Procrustes. It is the temptation of
symmetry and consistent logic. It is the temptation to sacrifice facts to
a scheme. A premature generalization from insufficient data yields
charming results, until some keen thrust reveals that "it is better not
to know so much than to know so much that is not so."

More and more, then, modern theology turns to that wholesome and
hopeful term, constructive. The constructive ideal, the constructive
method, are no new discovery of the present generation, though theology has moved into their atmosphere somewhat belatedly and not all
theologians are as yet equally aware of them. The familiar *a priori*
method of reasoning down from a few bold and sweeping generalizations
given to begin with is so much simpler than a painstaking building up
from tested data that it is entirely human to cling to it. The trouble—
—and a blessed trouble, too—is that the present generation will no
longer give us anything to begin with. It is unimpressed by "axioms"

concerning Almighty God; it will no longer grant that because He is infinite or perfect or transcendent He must necessarily think and act thus and so. The question is, Does He? Has He ever said that He does, or is there any indication of it in the facts? You do not know? Very well, then. First prove your premises, or else go humbly about the accumulation of data and the processes of sound inference as in any other department of thought that aspires to be called a science, let alone "queen of sciences."

More than most men realize, theology has been doing just that, and doing it for a long time past. There has been so much hue and cry about "dogmatism" on the one hand and "destructive scholarship" on the other, that the degree to which construction has not only been an ideal but has actually gone forward is lost sight of. There are those, of course, who, with new tools at their disposal, seem to take a certain ruthless pleasure in riddling the accepted and tearing down the familiar. But far more numerous are those who sound the genuinely constructive note, without which critical investigation, historical research, and exegetical light are after all pointless and ineffectual; and a noteworthy share of the best constructive work of our generation has in fact been done by men whose special studies lay in the field of criticism—which in their hands was no petty fault-finding—and of history—which proved to be far more than ancient dust. It were well if dogmatic theology could point to as many who press on with the like devotion and freshness of insight. And the minister who can preach in that fashion will find the pulpit still a throne.

Constructive interpretation is a primary need. There are data in abundance, long as their study was overshadowed by dogmatic custom. Would you understand, for example, the way of God with the soul, there is no need to take refuge in abstractions and assumed generalities. A measureless wealth of souls conscious of being loved by a heavenly Father, new-begotten through the work of a Saviour, illumined by an eternal Spirit, are at your hand—your own soul, your neighbor's, souls at worship in the church, souls in action in the market-place, souls self-portrayed in literature, souls living for all time in Holy Writ. Would you know the mind of God concerning sin, or character, or destiny, there is no need merely to conjecture what you would do or say if you were God, nor yet to thumb over the note-books of a dead professor. Has not God spoken? Does He not still speak? What are these deathless accents preserved by seer and saint, what this imperative of heart and conscience, what this majestic Christ who bodies forth the very being of the Eternal, and what this inward witness of the gracious Spirit? Oh! if we want a formula written out once for all, from which to deduce by mere syllogism a whole philosophy of being, I grant you I know not where to find it. But if we are willing to sit down reverently with the material that is at our hand in this Bible of ours and in the continuing Christian life in which we share, and prayerfully give ourselves to the guidance of promise, it is not the poverty of revelation that will stagger us but the wealth of it.

Time fails me to say more of all I would about theology's motives and objectives. Christ's two supreme commandments for daily living are the great commandments for theology, too—to love God (for theology by its very name revolves about Him) with heart and soul and mind and strength, and (the lesson so hard for theology to learn) to love one's neighbor as oneself. So impelled, let the theologian seek for truth, and not truth alone but clarity, and not clarity alone but quickening power. Whatever cold, inert, and academic studies you may conceive us to be cherishing on the hill yonder, the parish minister's theology must be a kindling flame, sprung from the world's Light and the Sun of righteousness, touching hearts, minds, and wills alike with heaven's pure fire.

Not only is there hope for a theology like that; it will itself be hopeful. Whence all this air of mustiness, this looking back, this lamentation of the departed past? There have been great ages of faith, and likewise shall be, but I know of no golden age of theology which demands reproduction in ours. The life is one and expanding. The truth is one and timeless. But the theology which thinks out the truth and interprets the life must be in some sense as new as the age to which it speaks. That is the very function of interpreters, to speak in living tongues, not dead. The God who is the source of life and truth has not left all the promise of growth and the joy of discovery to biologists, physicists, chemists, and astronomers. Before us also unknown worlds are spread. Within us also questions press for answer. "He shall guide you into all the truth" is the challenge to our expectancy, who still know in part and prophesy in part. And the theologian in pulpit and parish and study, side by side with the men of today in their struggle, hand in hand with the children in their trust, must not fail his people or his God. That we may know Christ, and that they may know Him, we press on.

X
Samuel M. Zwemer, 1876-1952

Dr. Zwemer, "apostle to Islam," graduated from New Brunswick in 1890. His career began with the founding of the Arabian Mission and led to a professorship at Princeton. An unflagging universal evangelistic vision marked his entire career. It applied especially to his burning desire to reach all Muslims, for whom he spoke and wrote, and with whose communities throughout the world he identified and visited. Representative of his thought on Christian mission is this chapter from *Into All the World* (1943).

What Constitutes a Call

All the prophets of the Old Testament and the apostles of the New Testament were deeply conscious of vocation. They were called of God; separated for a special task or mission; they were conscious of divine authority in their message. They were God's spokesmen.

Abraham (Gen. 12:1), Moses (Exod. 3:2), Gideon (Judges 6:11), Samuel (I Sam. 3:4), Isaiah (Chapter 6), Jeremiah, Ezekiel and Amos (7:14) are outstanding examples, although the circumstances of their call were diverse. Paul, too, was convinced of his vocation—that he was an apostle "not of men, neither by man" but "by Jesus Christ, and God the Father, who raised him from the dead" (Gal. 1:1). He begins many of his epistles by stating that he was called to be an apostle (Rom. 1:1, I Cor. 1:1; II Cor. 1:1; Eph. 1:1; Col. 1:1; I Tim. 1:1; II Tim. 1:1) and this call is "by the will of God" or "by the commandment of God our Saviour." Peter likewise refers to his call to be an apostle (I Peter 1:1; II Peter 1:1). John and Jude do not speak of their call directly but we read of it in the Synoptic Gospels. Jesus called the Twelve. Jesus chose and commissioned the Seventy. Paul considered his call and his conversion simultaneous. Then and there, on the way to Damascus, he was "separated unto the gospel" and commissioned to carry the Good News to the Gentiles. Three times he gives a circumstantial account of what took place. He "could not see for the glory of that light" . . . and he "was not disobedient unto the heavenly vision."

There is no doubt that in apostolic days men were called to apostolic tasks. The Acts of the Apostles tells the story from the day of Pentecost and Peter's vision on the housetop at Joppa, to the call that came to Timothy and Titus and Epaphroditus and Silas and Luke and Mark and all the others through human instrumentality but with divine power and distinctness.

No one doubts that Raymond Lull and Francis Xavier, William Carey and Henry Martyn, Adoniram Judson and John Paton, David Livingstone and Mary Slessor, Toyohika Kagawa and Hudson Taylor were each severally "called" to be God's missionaries. But what constitutes a call is a difficult question to answer. It is a practical question for every earnest Christian but especially for those in training for the Gospel ministry. Is there a special call for service across the seas? Is there a special call to non-Christian lands when we face today a non-Christian world? Does God still say as He did to Paul, "I will send thee far hence unto the Gentiles"?

No class of people faces these questions from a more practical standpoint than the students in theological seminaries. They are nearly all looking forward to the Gospel ministry. They discuss the question among themselves. They know the needs of the foreign field and its opportunities from their study of missions. They know something of conditions in non-Christian lands by their study of the great religions. Most of all, it becomes an urgent personal question, the answer to which is vital when we seek to know God's will. In reply to a questionnaire given to a group of students in Princeton Theological Seminary a few years ago, the following answers were characteristic. They may not be startling in their novelty, but they are encouraging in their discernment and meaning for the present generation of students. Among fifty replies there was none that expressed doubt of the necessity for a special call of God for the ministry, or implied that service abroad required no special qualifications. One hesitated as to whether a special call is needed to leave the homeland, saying:

"Complete consecration is the essential thing in a call. Thus every man who is wholly consecrated to Christ must consider where he can be of most service in bringing the kingdom on earth. Every Christian therefore has a call to the foreign field because the need there is so great. It would be more to the point to need a special call in order to stay in this country where the need does not seem so great."

A foreign student wrote: "In general there are two ways in which God calls to a certain work, whether that work be on the mission field or at home. He may speak to us directly through a vision, or we may hear His voice in our inner consciousness. This direct method is, however, rare in the present day—at least, not so common as a second method, namely, He brings about certain circumstances in our lives which determine a definite line of action. This method seems to be of two forms, which I shall call internal and external. In the internal instance, certain problems are raised which challenge human interest and thought. God calls us by illuminating our mind so that we are given insight as to the full significance of the problem, and He brings circumstances to bear upon our training and environment which fits us for that particular work.

"The call comes from an external stimulus when God directs outside factors to serve as stimuli, such as the advice of friends, parents, and others, or the reading of certain books, or God may touch our hearts by a speaker whose message is His call to us. Through my own experience I am sure that God's call is something very definite which is irresistible."

Another student emphasizes the idea, somewhat fancifully, that the various factors in a call are not easily determined: "As a man may fall in love in various ways, so is a man called to the mission field. Suddenly, or gradually, he realizes that there is nothing else worth while in life but this. God has ordained that he should do this. The reason for a call is neither emotional nor entirely a matter of reason, but a combination of both."

Another said: "The missionary call should be definite and dynamic in the life of the missionary. To my mind the sense of need in any land is not enough. People may be perishing; and there may be dire need for preaching and ministering in the name of Christ; yet these are not enough. The individual must have a sense of 'oughtness' in his own life or he won't be able to stand the challenge of the given field. A dynamic purpose, a sense of definite call must be experienced or the drive is lacking. Paul and Barnabas were good, wise preachers and ministers at Antioch, but it took a definite call of the Spirit to send them to the Gentile world."

Our last quotation is from an Oriental student pleading for his own nation and summing up the testimony: "What constituted the missionary call for Paul at Troas constitutes the missionary call today. It was the vision of a man voicing the needs of a nation and begging Paul: 'Come over and help us.' Paul could not resist the call and went over to help them. To those who love the Lord Jesus and who are willing to give their lives to His service and to His cause today, there comes the same vision—the vision of a nation yearning for Truth and Life. And when the vision comes, who can resist it?"

A careful study of how God called men and women to special tasks both in the Old and New Testament days as well as the actual experience of modern missionaries as recorded in their biographies, seems to show that there are three elements in a "call." First, there is the revelation of a great need for the salvation of God or of a special task to be performed for Him. This may come by vision or dream or study or by some providential guidance. Second, there is a sense of inadequacy, of inability or of an obstacle or difficulty that prevents acquiescence to God's call. And third, there is the removal of this hindrance by divine assistance or illumination. We have these three elements in the call of Moses, of Gideon, of Isaiah and of Jeremiah as well as in New Testament men; and yet how entirely different in other respects were their tasks and their environment. We would emphasize the fact that a sense of personal weakness or unworthiness is part of God's call. Humility and dependence on God are requisites for special service. This includes primarily the conviction that those whom God has saved from sin and death must tell others. "Woe is unto me, if I preach not the gospel." First, God calls to salvation, and then to service: "*Son,* go work today in my vineyard."

When God steps in to overcome Moses' reluctance, Gideon's fear, Isaiah's sense of sin, and Jeremiah's youthful timidity, they are each conscious of the presence of a Power not of themselves to enable them to undertake what seemed impossible.

The study of missionary biographies is proof that this is God's method of calling men to foreign service today. And what a fascinating study it is to trace a least common denominator in lives exceedingly different, talents utterly diverse, and labors exceptionally multiform. William Carey, Adoniram Judson, William Burns, David Livingstone, Alexander Mackay, Hudson Taylor, Albert Schweitzer—all of them heard the call, felt reluctant, unfit, or hindered by outward circumstance or inward heart-searching. And yet without doubt all were called and were faithful.

Perhaps we can best define an effectual call to service across the seas by modifying the Westminster Catechism definition of "effectual call" in the plan of salvation. It would then read: "It is the work of God's Spirit, whereby convincing us of the sin and misery of the non-Christian world, enlightening our minds in the knowledge of Christ's command and loving purpose to save mankind, He so renews our wills that we offer ourselves unreservedly for His service wherever His providence may send us."

In answer to such an effectual call George Grenfell went to the Congo, the better-known Grenfell to Labrador, Coillard to Basutoland, Pandita Ramabai to the widows of India, Verbeck to Japan, John Griffith to China, Allen Gardiner to Patagonia, Dr. Pennell to the borders of Afghanistan, Bishop Bompas to the Far North and Bishop Patterson to the South Seas, David Brainerd to the Delaware Indians and Van der Kemp to the Hottentots. Here we have the real apostolic succession and the continuation of the story of the heroes of faith given in the eleventh chapter of the Hebrews. Missionary biographies are a fascinating study, but should we attempt to refer all, time would fail us. Here is the story of two missionaries not widely known but whose influence in widely different spheres and fields of work was astonishing. Both were conscious of a definite call and through their life and death they are calling others today to the great task.

The first was W. Temple Gairdner of Cairo, Egypt; the other was Ingwer L. Nommensen of Sumatra.

On May 22, 1928, there entered into rest and the glorious life of the triumphant faithful one of the most distinguished leaders of missionary work in the Near East. From Cairo, as the center of his life activities, that wonderful spirit influenced wide circles far beyond Egypt, while in the great intellectual capital of the Moslem world his soul burned with the ardor of a star of the first magnitude in its intellectual brilliancy and the versatility of his genius.

Gairdner from his youth up had the best educational advantages, not only in a Christian home of culture and refinement, but in his preparatory studies and at Oxford. There he was soon distinguished as a scholar and he remained one all his life. He loved books and devoured them, but always with discrimination. The best Book of all books was therefore worthy of his most earnest study and most rigid spiritual discipline. While still an undergraduate he gave an address on "The First Duty of Students" which is a key to his own life:

"If once a man goes down from college without having acquired the habit of study, he will never acquire it. These years at college are our one chance. Often enough even studious men, who get caught into the busy whirl of a practical life, have perforce to drop this habit of study. But they can never lose the benefit of past habits . . . Why should Christians have narrow minds? What grace is there in them? None whatever. In fact, the very reverse. Have you never heard real unfairness in argument—a total want of sympathy with any point of view save the speaker's own—an ungracious intolerance, which makes one feel inclined to take sides against what one really believes? These are characteristics of the warped mind. And such minds are often produced by failure to study while at college. Let us be broad-minded in the true sense of that much misused, much-abused word."

One can judge how wide was the range of his scholarship by an incident that took place during the first World War. There were more than a score of Y.M.C.A. centers and camps for the armies in Egypt. Gairdner among many others was expected to lecture at Kantara for some days to the soldiers. In answer to a question about subjects, he sent the following list of topics from which to select:

"Mohammed; Mohammedanism; The History of Egypt, Ancient, Middle, or Modern; Modern Novelists and H. G. Wells; Ancient and Modern Cosmogonies (Early Systems of Astronomy and the Latest); The Causes of the War from Caesar to Kaiser (Race Movements and European History); Some Shakespearean Plays; Robert Louis Stevenson; The development and structure of Music; How the Hieroglyphics were deciphered." Such was the list on that half sheet of paper and he asked for half a day's notice before giving a lecture!

Judge from this the force, the grace, the versatility of the man who

proposed, mid the flies and tobacco smoke of a Y.M.C.A. hut, to talk
to newly enlisted men and veteran officers on such themes and yet hold
their attention. Gairdner, moreover, was not a naturally fluent speaker.
His manner of speech was often hesitating and his bodily presence was
sometimes against him. A friend at Oxford described him as "active,
vigorous, athletic, with a well-built figure but which he generally covered with unattractive and ill-fitting clothes." Who can forget seeing
him minus collar and necktie, on a bicycle reading a newspaper and
pushing the pedals to be on time at a committee.

With one great purpose in life, to exalt and preach Christ crucified,
Gairdner was careless of many conventionalities. He was too busy about
men's souls to spend much time on dress; his versatile mind, ever ready
to turn its attention in a new and unexplored quarter, could not fix itself
on the trivial things of life and sometimes seemed to wander far from
the obviously close at hand. This explains his frequent absent-mind-
edness. He was a good storyteller, an excellent companion, a skillful
musician (on the piano and the organ, which he often played simulta-
neously); he was also an artist in temperament, a dramatist and a poet
in English and Arabic. All of these gifts of genius he laid on the altar
of service for the King.

Here was a missionary who gave one short lifetime of service, in one
place, to one great idea—the evangelization of Moslems. He found his
lever and fulcrum in Cairo and set out to move a world.

His call to special service in Egypt came through a godly woman,
Miss Annie Van Sommer, at a summer conference, and her penetrating
word spoken in faith had results far beyond all expectation. He never
doubted it was God's definite, irrevocable summons to a great task.

Before he sailed for Egypt to work under the Church Missionary
Society he gave unstinted service to the Christian Student Movement
in Great Britain. He wrote three study textbooks on prayer and on the
Gospel of St. John; he won recruits immediately for service abroad; he
deepened spiritual life in the universities, for he had already come
under the influence of men such as John R. Mott, Robert P. Wilder and
Robert E. Speer. No wonder that he wrote:

"Our purpose must be, then to enter every college in the Kingdom,
and having entered it, win it wholly for Christ. Or, to put it into a
phrase, must not our aims be: to win the colleges for Christ, each of all
and all of each? . . . While our Unions are touching a mere set, as many
of them still are, and not reaching much of the strongest and best material at all; while men are not being won—and how few men are being
won!—while the very desire to win them, instead of burning like a fire

within the bones of those who profess Christ, is often cold, or sometimes positively does not exist—is our ideal realized?"

Gairdner's missionary ideals were lofty but sober. No one realized so keenly as he that the evangelization of Egypt was humanly an impossible task. He did not underestimate the strength of Islam, nor was he ignorant of the tremendous undertow in the surf for those who tried to save the lost. If ever a man travailed and toiled to bring a rescued man through the breakers, it was Gairdner. At his funeral some of these trophies of God's saving grace broke down in tears when they remembered what their salvation had cost him.

In his little book, *The Rebuke of Islam*, he stated truly that Islam was "the impossible-possible problem. For it is the only one of the great religions to come after Christianity; the only one that definitely claims to correct, complete and supercede Christianity; the only one that categorically denies the truth of Christianity; the only one that has in the past signally defeated Christianity; the only one that seriously disputes the world with Christianity; the only one which, in several parts of the world, is today forestalling and gaining on Christianity."

Face to face with such a problem, in the presentation of Christ, Gairdner was not only an earnest missionary but an able apologist and theologian.

All through his quarter of a century of service in Egypt, preaching, organizing, and dealing with many inquirers—the missionary found time (nay, took the golden hours) to write. The list of Gairdner's Arabic publications cover many fields of literature. Eleven tracts and books on Islam and Christianity came from his fertile pen and some of them were often reprinted and translated; all of them are increasingly valuable. He also wrote twelve books on Bible study and Bible biography; six on prayer and the devotional life, for Oriental Christians.

In the English language we have from his pen *The Life of D. L. Thornton, Edinburgh 1910, The Rebuke of Islam, Notes on the Epistle to the Romans,* and three important works on the Arabic language, its grammar, prosody and phonetics. In addition to all this he founded a Christian monthly Magazine in Arabic and English and was its chief editor for twenty-one years. Its circulation and support was his constant care, and, before his death, his pen was able to extend its influence in widening circles, from Alexandria to Khartoum and beyond.

It is, however, not the quantity but the quality of Gairdner's literary work that is astonishing. His *What Happened Before the Hegira?* is one of the most telling approaches to the Moslem mind ever written. The same is true of his *Death of the Perfect Man* as an interpretation of the very heart of the Atonement.

Most of all, this man of ten talents was a friend. He had the genius and the passion for making and holding friendships regardless of racial, social, or linguistic differences. His mind was international; he loved to bridge differences; he had a passion for Christian unity and felt personally humiliated when missionary groups or individuals failed to understand each other.

During the last months of Gairdner's severe illness, the circle of friends which surrounded him was composed of men, women and children, Syrians, Egyptians, Americans, Germans, Swedes, British, of every church and from among Moslems. At the funeral all Christian Cairo was represented—it was a common sorrow for the loss of a friend that brought so heterogeneous a company to the church and around the grave. Like Daniel, he was "a man greatly beloved."

Called of God, beloved of God and faithful unto death—yet if we count results in converts his harvest was only a handful of souls!

How different was the life of the German pioneer to Sumatra who reaped a rich harvest from a field ripe through earlier martyrdoms.

Ingwer Lodewijk Nommensen was a five-month-old infant when the American Baptist missionaries Lyman and Munson were murdered at Sibolga in 1834. His home was on a little island of the North Sea called Noordstrand, off the coast of Schleswig-Holstein. It was a home of desperate poverty. When scarcely more than a baby, Nommensen learned to linger at the homes of his little playmates until they had eaten, in order that he might obtain the scraps of food left on the plates. At the age of four, he crouched behind his mother while an angry rent-collector threatened and berated her. When he was eight years old he supplemented his mother's earnings by working as a shepherd during the summer months. At the age of ten he labored on a farm and did a man's work.

Two years later he was wrestling with some other boys beside the road and fell under the feet of a horse. The horse and the wheels of the carriage which he drew passed over the boy, crushing his leg. A year of intense suffering followed. Nommensen still longed to assist his mother. He learned to knit and sew and dragged himself about the hut preparing the food. A new teacher came to the school that winter and every day Nommensen's old schoolmates came to tell him the stories which the teacher had told them that day. These were stories of missionaries who had gone to far lands to take the message of the Gospel to those "who dwelt in darkness." The boy's heart burned within him as he listened. The Bible was the only book which his parents possessed and he read it avidly.

One day a doctor came to the island and visited the Nommensen hut.

He looked at the diseased leg and said, "His foot must be cut off as the bone is full of pus. It is the only way to save his life." Nommensen heard the words of the doctor but he felt that would defeat his life-plan. He opened his Bible and read:

"Verily, verily I say unto you. Whatsoever ye shall ask the Father in my name, He will give it you."

The boy pondered these words for a long time, and then called his mother.

"Mother, is it really so, that these words are true, even to this time?"

"Yes, they are true."

"Well, if they are, let us be zealous in asking from now on, that God heal my foot." He bowed his head and folded his thin little hands reverently as he prayed, "Oh God! Heal my foot!—and after that, send me to the heathen!" Six weeks later the people of the village were astonished to learn that the lad's foot was completely healed.

When Nommensen was nineteen years of age a rich woman adopted his youngest sister, and he was no longer needed to assist in the support of his family. He felt that the time had come to fulfil his promise to God. He bought a new Bible, a Testament, catechism and hymn book and prepared to go to the heathen.

He set out for Okholm where an uncle lived whose sons were sailors. He hoped they would take him to the heathen. But he had to wait long. In the meantime he had secured a good training for his life work. In June, 1861, he graduated from the seminary at Barmen, Germany, and in October of the same year was ordained a minister of the gospel. On December 24th, 1861, he sailed from Amsterdam, Holland, and *one hundred forty-two days later* reached Padang, Sumatra! Nommensen arrived in Sibolga on June 23rd, 1862, just twenty-eight years from the day on which Lyman and Munson left Sibolga to begin the journey to Silindung, which ended in their murder five days later. They were eaten by cannibals.

Nommensen started his journey to Silindung. He encountered many hardships on the journey and suffered from frequent attacks of malaria, but finally reached his destination. He was not welcomed by the Bataks of Silindung, however. Everywhere he met hostility and distrust and he was frequently ordered to leave. After long patience he won the heart of a Raja and built a house and small school on a small islet.

When Nommensen's house was completed he began to seek information concerning the murder of Lyman and Munson. When he learned that Raja Panggalamei, chief of their murderers, was still alive and dwelling in the little village of Sisangkak, he decided to take the Gospel to him. He reached the village in late afternoon and found the Raja's house enclosed by a bamboo hedge four meters high. He entered the enclosure quietly and motioned his Batak companions to wait outside in silence while he went into the house. Raja Panggalamei was seated by the fire. Thirty years had passed since the killing of Lyman and Munson and he had never seen another white man. When Nommensen entered and sat down beside him the Raja was stricken with terror and began to tremble violently and fled.

New trials awaited him but he preached until heathen hearts relented. At a great heathen feast the first break came. Many believed and were baptized. He labored on for fifty-seven years among these cannibal tribes. When he died in 1918 there were over 100,000 baptized Batak-Christians, fifty-five missionaries and over seven hundred native workers. This work of the Rhenish mission begun by Nommensen is one of the miracles of God's grace. Today there are over 300,000 Christians in Sumatra.

Who can doubt that the dauntless German lad with a crushed foot but uncrushed faith was called of God to be a missionary. In each case we have the three elements of an effectual call. And so many others were called, and are being called today. Called to preach the Gospel; to go into all the world; to finish the task of evangelism; to "occupy till He come."

Gairdner and Nommensen are striking examples of the effectual call of God to the foreign field. Even as Christ chose His apostles and called them to forsake all and follow Him; even as Paul was called to be an apostle and "separated unto the gospel," so God's Spirit and God's providence call and separate today.

When great multitudes followed Jesus, He turned and said to them: "If any man come to me, and hate not his father, and mother, and wife, and children, and brethren, and sisters, yea and his own life also, he cannot be my disciple. And whosoever doth not bear his cross, and come after me, cannot be my disciple" (Luke 14:25-27).

A generation ago, Robert E. Speer said to a great student convention: "The Evangelization of the World in this Generation is the summons of Jesus Christ to every one of the disciples to lay himself upon a cross, himself to walk in the footsteps of Him who, though He was rich, for our sakes became poor, that we through His poverty might be rich, himself to count his life as of no account, that he may spend it as Christ spent His for the redemption of the world."

"INTO ALL THE WORLD" signifies for each of us the world of our day, the post-war world of tomorrow. We must carry the good news to the most neglected and difficult fields, as well as to countries where the harvest is ripe and the call is for reapers in ever-increasing numbers.

The plea of destitution is even stronger than that of opportunity. Opportunism is not the last word in missions. The open door beckons; the closed door challenges him who has a right to enter. The unoccupied fields of the world have therefore a claim of peculiar weight and urgency. In this twentieth century of Christian missions there should be no unoccupied fields.

There are great and effectual open doors. And there are also gates of brass and bars of iron that remind us of many adversaries. But Jesus calls o'er the tumult of the present wild and restless world to follow Him.

Into All the World.
Pages 197-213.

XI

John W. Beardslee, Jr., 1879-1962

Dr. Beardslee is remembered by many of this generation with affection, and mimeographed copies of his classroom presentations still circulate among them. This brief article is from the *New Brunswick Theological Seminary Bulletin* of May, 1962.

The New Testament Doctrine of the Holy Spirit

Something happened at Pentecost. No one, not even the writers of the New Testament, has ever been able to find words with which to explain or even express the fact. The New Testament records are none too clear even in their dating of the great event. Luke tells of the coming of the Spirit upon the disciples fifty days after the Resurrection. The Fourth Gospel says that on the evening of the Resurrection day Jesus breathed upon the disciples and said to them, "Receive the Holy Spirit." Of one thing the early Christians were very sure. The risen Christ was with them. They were receiving from him a power unknown before. Their Christ could bestow this power because he was now risen. It had never been bestowed by God or Christ before that Resurrection. Different memories fixed upon different moments as the time of its first manifestation, but all were agreed that the Jesus who had seemed so futile, however lovely, needed this death and this inexplicable return in order to become able to bestow upon his loyal friends the new life which before his death was only a promise. They were now able to live as he had told them to live. Before his crucifixion his advice had seemed an idle dream. Now they found that his words had been true. Men could live his way and when they did so live they found it good. He was with them. His spirit was within them. They were living as he himself had lived. His Spirit was himself, no vague memory or inspiration but a real presence although the presence of a Spirit not the presence of a flesh and blood person. They found no distinction between the phrases "risen Christ" and the "Spirit of Christ." They were not two but one. Scholars once asked how it came to be that the Jesus of history became the Christ of the Church. But it is clear the Jesus of history and the Christ of the Church were never separate, the Christ was Jesus returned to his disciples, returned with a power which he had never before exerted. Something new had arrived. The Spirit of God was with them.

Something New Came Into the World

And yet the Spirit of God had always been active in the world. God's Spirit breathed upon chaos and an ordered universe appeared. God's Spirit enabled Samson to perform tasks beyond the power of simple humanity. God's Spirit told prophets what to say in rebuke or encour-

114

agement and the words spoken by the prophet became the very word of God to his people. The Spirit of God had functioned through the ages and yet Joel and Ezekiel announced it as in some sense lying in the future saying that God *would* pour out his Spirit and Jesus himself said that he *would* send the Spirit to his disciples. Furthermore, the Spirit's presence in the lives of God's people produced in the New Testament Church results quite different from the results of God's Spirit in the Old Testament story. Something new came into the world. The Spirit was now the Spirit 'of Christ as well as the Spirit of Christ's Father. God became man, we say. To save men God did the unbelievable. He became one of us, lived and died our kind of existence. This has always been the most difficult of New Testament truths to state or to defend or to accept. Not only the Resurrection of Jesus, but the life and death of Jesus as well need an explanation which has never been vouchsafed to the human mind. God came to men in the Spirit of the Risen Christ and thereby made himself available to common men and women as he had never been available before. The Spirit of Christ transformed people, made possible the new manhood of which Paul writes and the new birth of which Jesus spoke to Nicodemus. In Paul's letters the Spirit is different from the Spirit in Isaiah because in the time of Paul God in the incarnate Word had proved that he was superior to death, man's greatest and man's final enemy, and that now God would do what even he could not accomplish in his former separateness from man. Having become man he could bring man back to the normality in which he had created him. God comes to the Christian in the Church only in the Spirit of Christ, however true it is that no life has ever existed on the face of the earth except as it was sustained by the Spirit of God.

In the working out of a doctrine of the Trinity, a task with which the Church occupied itself for several centuries, the definition of the person and work of the Spirit gave much more trouble than the definition of the Father or of the Son. The human life of the incarnate Word offered a clear cut differentiation between Son and Father. One can put meaning into the phrase "God became man." To say that the Father became the Son has no meaning. The Church quickly arrived at what seemed an inevitable conclusion. Father and Son are equally God and yet are distinct. The Church could not refuse to attribute full deity to Christ because he was plainly producing within the Church results which could be produced by God alone.

The Holy Spirit the Spirit of Christ

With the Spirit the case was not so clear. The New Testament makes no distinction between the work of the risen Christ and the work of the

Holy Spirit or of the Spirit of Christ. Anything that can be done for the Christian or for the Church by whatever reality is represented by any one of the three phrases can be accomplished by either of the other two. And yet the New Testament frequently distinguishes between the risen Christ and the Spirit. This separation is most clearly seen in those places in which the Spirit is said to act in ways which imply a separate personality. The Spirit intercedes for the saints according to the will of God (Romans 8:27) and the searcher of hearts understands what the Spirit desires. In the closing chapters of the Fourth Gospel Jesus promises that he will return to his disciples after his death has parted him from them. He also tells them that he will send them the Spirit and that this Spirit will explain to them much about himself that was then obscure. The Church, basing its decision on its experience and on its understanding of the New Testament, concluded that here as in the more evident instance of Father and Son, there were both unity and difference. One could not refuse to attribute full deity to the Spirit nor could one refuse to allow the real distinction. To speak of the incarnation of the Spirit, for instance, made nonsense. Evidently, then, the doctrine of the Trinity is entirely dependent upon one's conception of the nature of the incarnate Jesus. Neither the Father nor the Spirit became man, but the incarnate Word is fully God. The Old Testament knows nothing of a doctrine of the Trinity. How could it? The Spirit which breathed on chaos or inspired Isaiah is thought of as the eternal God himself. Something new, (difficult as the thought must remain) was revealed concerning the Godhead when the Word became flesh, and that something new, continued to function when the bodily presence of Jesus was no longer present among men. Jesus himself remains with the Christian and with the Church. In some way which the human mind can neither understand nor express in language, Father, Son and Spirit are one and also three. For it must be remembered that the orthodox creeds are in no way meant to explain this mystery, however much friends and opponents of the Church have misconceived their purpose. The intelligent theologians of all the centuries have continually recognized that they were not penetrating to the depths of the mind of God. Among the last words of the New Testament to be written was the brief sentence, "No man hath seen God at any time." That was written long after men had walked and talked with the Christ and half a century after the Spirit of God had formed and guided the Church. The great creeds, even the horrible curses of the Athanasian Creed, were only intended to prevent the Church from denying or neglecting to acknowledge the various ways in which the eternal God was revealing himself and working out his purpose in the world. No creed attempts to reconcile these diversities. Human metaphors help, provided that the metaphors are not thought to be doctrinal statements. The spring, the stream, the river—water, ice, and steam, have proved useful as illustrations. But they offer only hints of the reality.

Jesus of Palestine Not Enough

A sentence of Basil the Great, one of the champions of orthodoxy, is worth quoting on this point. "As one who lays hold of a chain pulls the other end towards himself, so he who lays hold of the Spirit draws to himself through the Spirit the Son and the Father, and so if one truly receives the Son, the Son will bring with him on either hand the presence of the Father and of his own Holy Spirit, likewise he who receives the Father receives also in effect the Son and the Spirit. But the fellowship and the separation of the three are inexplicable and beyond our understanding." So far Basil. Since Jesus lived no one can receive the saving gifts of God except through Christ. We cannot leave Jesus out. But the mere human record of the thirty years of Jesus' life in Palestine will not bring us to God. God comes to us only by the Spirit which is the Spirit of Christ. The Jesus of Palestine is indispensable, but not enough.

It is through the Spirit of Christ alone then, that, since the Resurrection of Jesus, God has been working in the world and is now working. Note that this working of the Spirit is carried on only in the Church. No individual in the New Testament, except Christ himself, is ever said to have received the Spirit of God or the Spirit of Christ. The Spirit comes to individuals, but only as these individuals are embedded in the Church. Individuals have come forward professing to have been told by the Spirit that the Church is wrong or sinful. Now of course, individuals in the Church are often enough wrong or sinful. So are the human organizations in which we, as human beings, can alone express the life and carry on the activity of the Church universal. But the Church of Christ is never wrong or sinful and for any human being to profess himself gifted with a revelation superior to that of the Church merely reveals the petty conceit of such an individual. Every Christian must always check a supposed guidance of the Spirit by the guidance that Spirit is offering to other members of the Church of Christ. No one of us dare go on our solitary way pretending that we alone are favored with the presence and help and direction of the Spirit. True, the Spirit directs different individuals to different tasks, different ideas, and different ways of working, as Paul so eloquently insists in First Corinthians 12, but Paul also points out that these differing directions are all the work of the same Spirit, who never contradicts himself and who never leads any Christian to contradict the guidance offered to another. The Spirit works only with individuals and only with the Church, another distinction difficult to state in terms of human logic, and still more difficult to practise while rigidly maintaining the courtesy due one's neighbor and the loyalty due one's Christ. An excessive individuality within the Church, the unwillingness to cooperate with others, has too frequently been defended as the inspiration of the Spirit.

Two Gifts of the Spirit

Just what does this Spirit of Christ offer the member of Christ's body, the Church, which that member can receive from no other source? Two gifts. Guidance and Power.

The teaching of Jesus in the Synoptic Gospels is without doubt final. Strange indeed that so many of the professed hyper-orthodox should disparage that teaching or relegate it to some phase of life other than the present. I remember hearing a New York preacher once warn his Church members against ever repeating the Lord's Prayer, because that teaching was not meant for the Church. It would seem that the more genuinely one accepted the full deity of Jesus the more intently one would heed his words. But, however divine the teaching of Jesus is, it forms no new law imposed on either the Church or the world. All law is abolished with the Gospel. Although, then, the teaching of Jesus is God's own inspired direction, showing his people how he wants them to behave towards one another and how alone they may achieve happiness and success, that teaching must be interpreted in order to direct the particular situations and emergencies of daily life. Just because these words of Jesus are so supremely important, their misuse and their misapplication can become desperately destructive. To the Christian in the midst of these perplexities comes the Spirit of Christ. He tells us nothing new, nothing contradictory to the words of Jesus, but he explains to individuals or groups within his Church how to use and apply the wonderful words of life which he spoke to hesitant and doubting groups in Galilee and Jerusalem.

He Died to Make Us Good

But to know the way of life is not enough. Even to choose that way, to determine to live it, to align ourself with Jesus is not enough. One

of the saddest features of the long tale of human effort throughout the
centuries is the repeated failure of good men to produce good acts. We
all know how we resolve to do what we know to be good and find that
our action has been recreant to our good determination. Humanity is
too weak to perform what it knows to be good. Into this situation came
Jesus. He died to make us good. His Spirit controls the weak wills of
his people and enables them to succeed where they had proved themselves incompetent without him. One of the most touching pictures in
all the Bible is the description, in the early chapters of the Acts, of the
disciples' surprise at discovering that they were actually living as Jesus
had told them they should. His words, what we call his teaching, had
seemed puzzling and impossible. They could not see what so wonderful
a character could mean by telling them that God's chief requirement
was a peaceful comradeship with one another and an utter devotion to
one another's welfare without regard to one's own personal desires or
satisfactions. And now that he had died and had come back to them,
now that his Spirit was present with them, they found that they were
living together in precisely the way which he prescribed. Is it not true
that for nineteen hundred years the actual performance of Christian
people united in Christ's Church has been the wonder of themselves
and of outsiders. Christian people have lapsed enough. But the lapses
are recognized to be not the result of the power of Christ's Spirit, but
the results of the neglect and the abandonment of that Spirit. We ought
to deplore the deficiencies of Christian people. We ought not to apol-
ogize for the actual performance of the Christian Church. Not only has
God's guidance come to that Church through the Spirit of the risen and
present Christ, but the Spirit has so entered the lives of the members
of the Church as to enable them to achieve a service and a love un-
dreamed of outside the Christian circle and impossible of attainment
without the presence of the Spirit.

Controlled by the Spirit of Christ

Some thirty times Paul uses the word "pneumatikos," usually translated even in the best versions by the English word "Spiritual." We
read of a "Spiritual gift," a "Spiritual blessing," a "Spiritual body," a
"Spiritual food," of "Spiritual persons," or a "Spiritual law." It seems to
me that the ordinary translation of this word is both inadequate and
misleading. If the word Spiritual means anything to the people in our
pews it means non-material or ghostly. A spiritual person is thought of
as some ancient saint whose interests have no longer anything to do

with earth but whose mind is fixed on heaven. Nothing could be farther
from Paul's meaning. If the word "pneumatikos" should always be translated "controlled by the Spirit of Christ" our people might grasp Paul's
meaning. A spiritual person is not an unworldly person. He is one whose
words and deeds in the world are guided and controlled by the Spirit
of Christ. A spiritual gift is an endowment given by Christ's Spirit which
fits one for a special task. The task may be wholly worldly, collecting
money, for instance.

Spiritual wisdom is the kind of wisdom which we receive from the
Spirit of Christ or go without. A spiritual body is a personality wholly
mastered by Christ's Spirit, the kind of personality which Paul expects
in another life and knows that he has not yet attained. A spiritual law
is law interpreted by Christ's Spirit. The use of the English adjective
spiritual in these important passages conceals the fact that in them Paul
is always writing of the personal impact of Christ upon the believer.
The Spirit is doing for the believer what the believer cannot do for
himself. When I succeed, says Paul, it is not I, but the Christ within
me, that is his Spirit, that succeeds.

And this Spirit is never in the New Testament thought of as an abstraction, like the Spirit of Shakespeare or the Spirit of the times, or
the Spirit of '76. Nor is it that "mind of the universe" which in Greek
poetry and philosophy, as in Wordsworth, pervades all things. The Spirit
with which Paul and Jesus are filled is always the Spirit of the personal
Christ—Jesus himself, with them more really than he was ever with
Peter in Galilee, interpreting to each within his Church the mind and
the will of God in whatever situation may be present. The Church's
future, like the individual's future, is wholly dependent on obedience
to this Spirit. What he will plan or what he will direct no one can know
or foresee. We know that the past and the present will not guide us for
the future. Something different is in store, for he is a living Master and
not a dead Teacher. But we also know that no Spirit-guided future will
contradict the human Jesus who during his life on earth never once
failed to do the will of his Father in heaven.

XII

Abraham J. Muste, 1885-1967

A. J. Muste, class of 1909, served his first pastorate in the Fort Washington Collegiate Church. He is well known as a social activist. Before achieving national and international fame as a peace activist, Mr. Muste had pioneered in labor activism and in labor education, serving largely outside the Reformed Church as a Congregationalist and as a Presbyterian. He has recently been highly honored by Hope College, his first alma mater, and by New Brunswick. "War Is the Enemy" was written in 1942 and is from the volume, *The Essays of A. J. Muste.*

War Is the Enemy

It would be pertinent at this time to explain the underlying philosophy of those who, in the face of the present world situation, hold to the way of nonviolence, with a view toward clarification rather than argument. It is a prerequisite of fruitful thought and discussion in such a crisis that we should think of each other, pacifists and non-pacifists, as fellow-searchers for truth, not as intellectual adversaries. In each of the diverse positions which men hold there will be something that is valid, that represents an effort to respond to the situation, a fidelity to the truth as they see it. Recognizing this is a way of achieving at-oneness with our fellows.

At-oneness, however, must not be confused with appeasement. The truth is often hard and harsh. There is sometimes a tendency, therefore, to refrain from stating issues sharply and clearly, to gloss over differences, perhaps on the pretext that "our agreements are so much greater than our differences after all," and that bringing out the issues and facing them "does not make for reconciliation." Similarly we often hear it said that in the church or religious meeting, or elsewhere, "controversial issues" ought not to be discussed.

Grave dangers may lurk behind these plausible suggestions. No reconciliation—within a single human soul, between man and wife, in a family, an industry, a nation, or between nations—was ever built on a lie or a half-truth. "Ye shall know the truth, and the truth shall make you free"; conversely, aught but the truth leads to slavery and strife. Have we not all experienced this many times? What a healing coolness and balm come into any situation the moment nobody is pretending any more, nobody is holding anything back. Even though it be a very difficult situation, the poison has been sucked out of it when those involved speak their minds freely.

For the individual, salvation, reconciliation with God, begins with the bitter experience of facing the truth about himself, shedding all pretense and evasion, and crying out, "God, be merciful to me, a sinner." In our relations with one another, although it ill becomes us to try to beat our version of the truth into our neighbor's brain with arguments, we owe it to him to bear faithful witness to the truth as we see it, holding nothing back and in nought equivocating. And any parent knows that making oneself agreeable to a child is not the same as loving him.

Sometimes, behind our reticences, there is a subtle snobbishness, a feeling of "why bother to discuss with him or tell him what I think: he wouldn't understand anyway." There is no greater honor a man can pay his fellows, no greater service he can render them, than to share with them such truth as has been vouchsafed to him. And, as for the proposal to avoid "controversial issues," usually it amounts to a counsel of despair, for if an issue is a real one there are bound to be differences of opinion; it is bound to be "controversial."

Much the same observations apply to proposals that a moratorium be declared on the discussion of certain matters for a certain time—for example for the duration of the war—and that during this period pacifists should devote themselves exclusively to "works of mercy and healing." That pacifists should be not mere talkers, but practical friends and helpers, and especially in wartime, can hardly be too often or too emphatically stated. We have no desire to obstruct our fellow citizens in the performance of what they regard as their patriotic duty. "There is a time for silence," and probably many of us talk too much. We are not all called to perform the same tasks in the same way. Nor must we press impatiently for immediate results, like the child who sows his seeds one day and digs them up the next to see if they are sprouting. Having given witness to the truth as best we can, we must be content to let it make its own way in the minds and hearts of men.

But the idea that in wartime there might be a general moratorium on the preaching of our philosophy and gospel, including their application to the immediate concrete situation, and that this somehow would make for reconciliation, seems to me unsound. Let us suppose that the religious-pacifist analysis of war, of its effects, of its evils, is suspended. Obviously that does not mean that people will have no other ideas presented to them, that no analysis of current developments is attempted. It does mean that what the religious pacifist regards as false and dangerous ideas are presented, but no criticism and no alternatives. Why should we regard such conduct as democratic, or as loyal on our part to our fellows? We hope that some day men will experience a great revulsion against war, will lay down their arms, and cease to trust those who advocate or acquiesce in the method of war. If in that hour we try to tell them of a better way will they not ask, "Why did you keep still while we were engaged in senseless slaughter? And why should we have any special confidence in you who took pains to keep your counsel until everybody agreed with you?"

Surely the time to witness against tragic, self-righteous distortion of the truth is at the moment when it is widely proclaimed and believed. Moreover, silence and passivity in the presence of falsehood, injustice and oppression, and the waging of war, is likely to mean that for a momentary and delusive sense of unity with our "own folk" we pay in the coin of alienation from the victims of injustice and from God's children on the other side of the border. And the reconciliation with our own people is certain to be temporary and unreal; we have not really done them a service when, by our silence, we permit the impression to stand, for example, that we acquiesce in the version of the Japanese mentality and character which prevails in so many American circles today. For what men need is not that other men should agree with their ideas or be indulgent toward them. What they need to save them from "the hell of fire" is to be able to believe in themselves, in truth, in an inexorable moral order, in the God of Love. Men always have been helped so to believe by the sight of men who were true to themselves, who refused to blunt "the Word of God which is a two-edged sword," who could "hate" father, mother, wife, child, their own life, for God's sake. These men, though in their life they may have been rejected and crucified, have always been the great reconcilers, the centers around which human societies were built.

Often it is true we cannot speak or act where conflict rages and evil is being done, because we do not love enough. We know that our eye is not single, that we are not disinterested, that we desire the satisfaction of setting somebody right rather than the right itself. It is true that while we are in this condition we cannot speak, or that if we do, we merely bungle or destroy; our only course, then, is to change our condition.

The reconciliation which must take place in our own minds and spirits, whether we be pacifists or non-pacifists, is promoted when we try to think through each problem with our fellows with something of that innocence and freshness and childlikeness and humility which, Jesus taught, is the gateway to truth and felicity. In other words, in each moment we seek to divest ourselves of any notion that our knowledge is sufficient and final; of prejudices; of inappropriate emotions. The moment we find resistance and resentment against an idea stiffening our mental attitude, stridency creeping into our voices, we should examine ourselves. It will be the signal that there is something in that idea which we have not yet been willing to take fully into account. Our highly emotional "certainty" that it is absurd will really mean that deep down we are not sure of our own position.

Our unwillingness to be reconciled to truth, which is a manifestation of God, to accept it in its fullness and with our whole mind ("Thou shalt love the Lord thy God with all thy mind") is one of the fundamental causes of division in life, of the divided self, the divided human family. On the other hand, almost nothing can do so much to increase our spiritual health and power, our effectiveness in the work of reconciliation, as to discipline ourselves to discern and renounce our prejudices. When we think of our insights as having finality, as something to be possessed and defended, we set up a wall against God who is the Source of Light and whom we can receive only if we become infinitely receptive like little children.

Now in the degree that we have divested ourselves of inner resistance to the truth and have developed a readiness to receive it from whatever source, we are also enabled to "speak the truth—in love." We can hope that our fellows may see and come to welcome the light that we have. And we can let our testimony go forth, let our light shine, and not, out of a secret cowardice or false modesty, which is also "self-propitiation" and self-indulgence, put our light "under a bushel, but on a stand so that it may shine to all that are in the house."

It does not, however, follow that disinterested love invariably wins an immediate and predictable victory. That has not, alas, been the Eternal Father's experience with us; and in this as in other respects, "the servant is not above his Master." There is no reconciliation through the medium of any partial love, but only through a love that is prepared to pay the final price, which lasts unto and through death. The final price is not always required; often it is, and always the readiness to pay must be clearly demonstrated. Certainly, until individuals and nations are prepared to sacrifice as much in practicing reconciliation and non-violence as they sacrifice in the pursuit of war, we cannot reasonably expect an end of wars. It is a fact, as well established as any in history, that human enmities are healed and human communities are built through the process of costing, sacrificial love. The apostle Paul spoke, not of a remote theological dogma but of this demonstrable truth when he wrote to the Ephesians: "Ye that once were far off are made nigh *in the blood of Christ.*" He who would save men and heal strife first must unite in himself both reconciliation and a new order. He must "create in himself, of the two, one new man, so making peace and reconciling both in one body unto God through the cross, *having slain the enmity thereby.*" To what as yet uncalculated sacrifice, in prayer, in giving, in witnessing, in renunciation of war, in service to human need, are we called in order that in us the world's enmity may be slain!

From this vantage point, then, let us consider for a moment the problems confronting our own nation and all the world's peoples in this grim hour. Many sincere persons are saying: "We are faced with a

terrible dilemma, a choice of diabolical evils. We know what it means
to resort to war, war under modern conditions and with modern weapons, war on the planetary scale which is required to stop Hitler and the
other aggressors. We recognize that we share to a large extent in responsibility for things having come to their present pass. But, as things
stand now, we cannot believe that anything except decisive defeat in
war can stop the sweep of the utterly inhuman, brutal dictatorships.
The possibility of a hegemony of Nazi might and the Nazi philosophy
of life over the world, over our own children, for a generation, many
generations, possibly centuries, seems to us an evil so monstrous that
it is better to resort to war on the chance that we may prevent it than
to stand aside from the conflict. We have no illusions about war or about
our own superior virtues; therefore we believe that we can fight without
bitterness and hate. If, by the grace of God, we win, we shall make a
wiser, more Christian use of our victory than we made the last time.
We believe the English-speaking world has learned a bitter lesson as a
result of the last war and of the peace which we lost following that war.
We shall not make those mistakes again."

It would require a whole book even to begin to deal with all the
problems presented here. We must therefore confine ourselves to a
brief statement of what seem the basic elements in religious-pacifist
criticism of this position. We take the points in the preceding paragraph
in reverse order so as to come last to the most fundamental issue.

In the first place, we believe that it is a dangerous delusion to think
that if the United States and its allies were to win, we should make a
much better use of our opportunity than we did the last time. This
argument assumes that the course followed ever since the last war was
a major factor in bringing on the outbreak of the present war. Yet, since
the outbreak of war in 1939, the United States has followed step for
step a course similar to that followed in 1914-1917. The result is that
we are again completely involved in total, world-wide war. Every indication seems to point to our following the same familiar pattern from
this point on, i.e., to aim at a decisive military victory, one which indeed
will cripple our national enemies much more completely and give us a
much greater relative superiority than before. But we tell ourselves
that, having arrived with fatal precision at that point, a miracle will
happen. The momentum acquired in the terrific plunge downhill into
which the nations are pouring all their energies will disappear as if by
magic. We shall suddenly get off this road and strike out boldly in
another direction. What reason have we to believe this? Surely we have
a right to ask for concrete evidence.

When we examine that concrete evidence, I think we find either that it is very shaky or that it points in quite the opposite direction. For example, men cite the better treatment of conscientious objectors and the extent to which civil liberties are being preserved in Britain and the United States. But it cannot be denied that these things occur within a general context of increasing concentration of power in the executive, regimentation of the entire population, and the gearing of all energies to war purposes, and that it is these developments that are decisive. Furthermore, the period after a great war is always one of catastrophic spiritual let-down; and we see no good reason for supposing that it can be otherwise this time.

Will those who write the peace this time, whoever they are, have more favorable conditions with which to work than did Wilson and Lloyd George? To ask the question is to answer it in the negative, though it is safe to say that few have even tried to imagine and none can really visualize what conditions will be after many more months, or years, of war and blood-letting; after the subjugated peoples of Europe turn upon the Germans and wreak vengeance upon them (avowedly a part of Allied strategy); after pestilence, famine, social chaos have done their work. If the job of policing the situation proved too much after the last war and ended in the debacles of 1929 and 1939, what reason to expect a different result now?

Furthermore, responsible leaders quite frankly pitch their objectives much lower than did the statesmen of the last war and of the "peace." Their frankness may be to their credit, but we cannot safely discount the significance of their announced aims. So able and temperate an expert in international affairs as John Foster Dulles has said of the Atlantic Charter: "In its present form, it falls far short of the conceptions of President Wilson, and *short even of their expression in the Treaty of Versailles.*" During the last war, we said that we must disarm Germany and that we too must promptly disarm, since not to do so could only mean further war. This time, our statesmen frankly say that we do not think in terms of no more war following the present one; that we must disarm "the aggressors" even more completely than before; "make it impossible for them to raise their heads ever again," while we remain "suitably protected." This can only mean American-British military domination of the earth. It seems to us to require a grave arrogance, or a great simplicity, to suppose that in the context of the post-war situation this can spell aught but disaster for us and for mankind. Altogether the prospect for a "better peace" is scarcely so promising as to constitute a convincing reason for participation in war.

In the second place, a word about the contention that war can be waged without hate and bitterness. People come back from England

and report that they have not encountered a single trace of these emotions. It may be that our penchant for seeing and hearing what we want to see and hear plays a part here. Certainly expressions calculated to stir up hate and contempt for a people are not absent from Mr. Churchill's references to Germans. Dr. Arthur Salter, M. P., stated in the House of Commons recently: "Open retaliation and revenge are now being advocated in the highest quarters. No apologies are being offered for the indiscriminate bombing of women and children. Now we have photographs showing whole streets of working-class houses being blown sky-high by our bombs." It is evident that hatred for the Japanese has been fairly general in the United States in recent weeks. The training in our military forces is not based on the theory that teaching our young men to love their enemies is the best way to make good soldiers of them.

If it is true that people do all that modern warfare requires without being aware of any emotions of hate and anger, feeling quite composed and virtuous and "sweet," it is evident that we are faced with a grave psychological and moral problem. This would not be the first time that such a phenomenon has been witnessed. The men who tortured and killed the victims of the Inquisition did so "for the greater glory of God," and out of compassion, in order to save the souls of those victims! The amazing and dangerous situation into which we may now be moving was suggested by the columnist who recently urged that we need not grow hysterical with hate as we did in the last war, and went on to say that, while it might become a military necessity to blot out whole Japanese cities by bombing from the air, we should do so calmly and objectively, with no poison of hate in our hearts. But what has happened here? As Professor Harper Brown, of Wellesley, pointed out in a recent discussion, a complete splitting of personality has taken place. There is no relationship between what men feel and what they do. If this process continues there will be no limit to the deeds we may perform, the havoc that may be wrought, while all the time we experience no inner turmoil, feel quite composed, even congratulate ourselves on the fact that we do not experience the emotions which in ordinary mortals accompany the performance of acts of destruction, deceit and killing. Under other circumstances that would be regarded as an advanced form of insanity. Perhaps the ordinary mortal who is not free from rages and hate when performing the acts of a soldier is, after all, a better integrated personality and nearer to a state of grace, whether from the standpoint of the psychologist or of the gospel. And what will be the personal and the social reactions as the divorce between inner state and outward act becomes more complete—and in that hour of awakening and return to

reality when men contemplate with unveiled eyes what they have done
"for the greater glory of God" and in "love" for their enemies?

We come thus to the most crucial question. Men of goodwill recognize
how terrible is the dilemma, but choose war because, in spite of everything, it seems the only way to prevent the establishment of a diabolical,
demoniacal tyranny over all men, the only chance to build a decent
world again. Here, we are face to face with the problem of calculating
the consequences of our decisions and actions in complex social situations; and at this point all of us, pacifists and non-pacifists alike, suffer
from the limitation that we are human and fallible and can see only a
short distance ahead and calculate only a few of the consequences of our
decisions, and these only imperfectly. Political campaigns and wars and
treaty-making seldom are what they appear to be or accomplish what
the actors in them professedly or actually seek to accomplish. If, therefore, non-pacifist friends assert that I may not be fully aware of the
consequences of my refusal to support the United States government
in war, I readily agree that this is so. But neither can they calculate the
consequences of their actions; certain it is that in helping to release the
terrible forces of modern warfare, they release forces over which they
have no control, and to judge by the experience of the last war, they
may live to regret the consequences bitterly.

Are we then utterly without guide and compass in this wilderness?
Are we condemned to mere guess-work? Aldous Huxley has given an
answer to that question in his remarkable recent book, *Grey Eminence:*
"It is by no means impossible to foresee, in the light of past historical
experience, the *sort* of consequences that are likely, in a general way,
to follow certain *sorts* of acts. Thus, from the records of past experience,
it seems sufficiently clear that the consequences attendant on a course
of action involving large-scale war, violent revolution, unrestrained tyranny and persecution are likely to be bad."

Another way to put the answer would be to point out that, in the
more restricted realm of personal relationships, we are guided by our
moral codes and moral impulses. We do not deceive, steal, assault,
blackmail, even though it looks as if the immediate consequences in a
specific situation might be favorable. Whether we think of moral codes
and impulses as expressions of an objective moral order or simply as
representing what the race has found by experience to be good in the
long run, does not in this connection make any important difference.
The point is that, in a real sense, conscience, the Inner Light, is the
only guide among the complexities of life. What we know surely, and
the only thing we can know, is that evil cannot produce good, violence

can produce only violence, love is forever the only power that can conquer evil and establish good on earth.

Here I bear witness for a moment out of personal experience. Like most of the others in the small Christian pacifist group during the last war, I was ill-informed about economics and politics, utterly unsophisticated. Now, when I hear my non-pacifist friends, including many who consider themselves conservative and substantial citizens, talking about "choice between evils," and the need of being "realistic," when I hear them say that we must first get the situation in hand by violence and only then can we set about building a brave new world, I can close my eyes and feel that I am hearing the communists who, for a time, converted me to Marxism-Leninism!

Two things emerged out of my experiences, as pacifist and later as Marxist-Leninist, which greatly influence my outlook today. The pacifists of the last war, ill-informed and unsophisticated though we were, somehow sensed what the war was really about, sensed the unreliability of the war propaganda, sensed what would come after the war. Later, when I had ceased to be a pacifist, I became much better informed. But presently I found that, although I was much more experienced in analyzing what lay just ahead and taking the next step, my grasp of the total development in my own life and in the world became more and more fumbling; I drifted into a complete opportunism which brought outward confusion and inner disintegration. The only explanation I have for this experience is this: the law that evil can be overcome only by its opposite, i.e., by a dynamic, sacrificial goodness, is so basic in the structure of the universe, so central for an understanding of life and history, that if one stands at that center he sees things in clear focus. He may not know much, but that much he will see clearly. Contrarily, if one moves away from that center, he may know and see vastly more, but it will be out of focus, blurred.

Secondly, Lenin taught me that if you are going to be "realistic," you must be thoroughly realistic. If the success of your movement may depend on violence applied effectively at the right moment, then it is criminal to prepare "too little and too late." You must accustom your people to the idea of violence, you must acquire weapons. Since in war the offensive may be the best defense, you must be ready for that too. From this experience I became convinced that, in spite of all the brains, the vast energies, the titanic sacrifices that went into the revolutionary movement, the effort to establish democracy by dictatorship, brotherhood by terrorism and espionage, fullness of life by war and violence, would leave you with dictatorship, terrorism and strife, not with the fair goals of which men had dreamed. The end could not be divorced from the means; the means thwarted and corrupted the idealistic end. All the leading early revolutionists in Russia, except Lenin and Stalin, were liquidated by assassination or exile; no fewer than three million peasants were destroyed in the forcible collectivization of agriculture, and the Russians are so far from having achieved the classless society of which ancient seers and modern revolutionists and proletarians dreamed that an analysis of statistics published in the Soviet press reveals that the upper eleven or twelve percent of the population receives approximately half of the national income. (This differentiation is even sharper than in the United States, where the upper ten percent receives approximately 35 percent of the national income.) Demoralization and defeat overtook the modern revolutionary movements in all other important centers also, as for example in Germany, often spoken of as "the classic land of Marxism," where the degeneration of the whole movement of social protest and revolt had gone so far that when Hitler came to power it did not offer even a gesture of resistance, violent or nonviolent.

Few would question the analysis of the relationship between means and ends in this case. In the 1920s and 1930s, people were practically unanimous in pointing out that World War I had failed miserably to accomplish what good people had believed it would; and college faculties still contain many members who are troubled about the "souls" of their students, because the students still believe what the professors told them about war a few years ago. Again we ask: what reason have men to believe that, "this time," it all will be different?

So much for the negative side of our position. Now for the positive proposals.

It is significant that friends who have often said to us, "Almost thou persuadest me to be a pacifist," now are saying that a great deal of thought must be given at once, even though the war so far as the United States is concerned has only begun, to the problem of "a just and durable peace." It is inevitable that reasonable and conscientious men should feel this concern, for obviously the only justifiable end of war is a "good peace," a peace that does not sow the seed of future war. Unless men can believe in such a goal, war, wholesale slaughter, becomes utterly irrational and completely immoral. It would then, beyond a shadow of doubt, be "the sum of all evils."

We have already stated our disbelief in the likelihood that we can follow the same fatal path as in the last war and then, suddenly, at the moment of victory for "our side," strike out in an entirely new direction to a durable and tolerable, not to mention a noble, peace. Before the United States entered into war, the religious pacifist could only say: "Go not to war, keep the sword in its scabbard; instead of drifting into war, take the initiative in offering to the world a creative, dynamic peace, a way out of this fearful impasse of a military victory for this Axis or that." It seems to me the only thing we can say to our nation now is: "Stop the war, put up your sword before it is too late altogether. Instead of automatically going through the old motions, be imaginative, be creative. There is no hope in a peace dictated by 'totalitarian' powers; nor in a peace dictated by 'democratic' powers. That has already been tried and proved disastrous. We are incurring stupendous risks in trying that course once more; let us rather take some risks for a new course. O, our country, pioneer again—this time on a world scale; for mankind's sake, try the way of reconciliation."

In political terms, such a policy would express itself in an offer by the United States to enter into negotiations immediately with all nations, Axis and Allies, based on such terms as the following:

1. The United States will take its full share of responsibility, with other nations, for the building of federal world government along such lines as those of our American union.

2. Instead of seeking to hold on to what we have, which is so much more than any other people have, the United States will offer to invest the billions which otherwise it would devote to war preparation and war, in a sound international plan for the economic rehabilitation of Europe and Asia, and in order to stay the inroads of famine and pestilence which otherwise threaten to engulf mankind.

3. In the coming peace no attempt shall be made to fasten *sole* war-guilt on any nation or group of nations. Instead, all people should take up the works of repentance in a common effort to halt the break-up of civilization and to build the good life which the earth's resources and modern technology make possible for all.

4. All subject nations, including India, the Philippines, Puerto Rico, Denmark, Norway, France, Belgium, Holland, and subject peoples on every continent, must be given a genuine opportunity to determine their own destinies. In those few cases where a people are clearly not yet ready for self-government, their affairs should be administered by the federal world government with a primary view to the welfare of such people and to the granting of full self-determination at the earliest possible time.

5. All peoples should be assured of equitable access to markets and to essential raw materials. To this end, concerted action to adjust and ultimately to remove tariff barriers should be undertaken. Immigration and emigration should be internationally controlled with a view to the welfare of every nation. There is a direct and

infinitely tragic connection between (a.) the fact that since 1914 there has been no *free* movement of population and labor from one country to another and (b.) the *forcible* uprooting of millions by brutal discriminatory legislation and by war. Stifle immigration and you get refugees.

6. To give a lead in furthering democracy, the United States will undertake to establish equality of opportunity for all within its own borders: to begin with, a national program should be established to provide decent housing for all who now lack it; to make unused land accessible to those who will till it; to encourage cooperatives for the maintenance and revival of the initiative of our people; to provide adequate medical and hospital service and equal educational facilities for all, including Negroes and Orientals.

7. The United States will repudiate every form of racism in dealing with all minority groups and, as an initial move toward reconciliation in the Far East, repeal the Oriental Exclusion Act. It will call on Germany and other countries similarly to renounce racist doctrines and practices.

8. There should be immediate and drastic reduction of armaments by all nations, and steps to move from an armaments-and-war economy to an economy of peace should be taken as rapidly as possible.

We readily admit that, from the standpoint of "power politics," national aggrandizement—any materialistic interpretation of history—this seems a fantastic proposal. But any proposal made by idealistic non-pacifists seems to us quite as untenable. They believe, for example, that a wedge ultimately must be driven and can be driven between the German people and Hitler and Hitlerism. There can be no good peace, they say, until the demons have been driven out of the souls of the German people. For the present, however, they believe that military means must be used to that end. But to say to the German people: "The world has no realistic choice except a military victory, decisive, crushing, of your side or our side" is to tell them the same thing that Hitler tells them. This is what keeps them fighting behind Hitler, as practically all observers admit; for, on that basis, they believe that the only alternative to a victory behind Hitler is "something worse than Versailles." They might as well keep on fighting, since they face hell in any case and there remains the outside chance that they might win and then let the rest of the world find out what it means to be the underdog. There is, furthermore, the ghastly record of what our "success" in separating the German people from the Kaiser by military means amounted to: it gave us Hitler in place of the Kaiser.

This brings us to another dilemma. Our proposal for a dynamic peace at this time is dismissed by non-pacifists as "unrealistic." It would require an impossibly great change of heart in the German people and others. The American people, too, would have to rise to heights of repentance, faith in spiritual forces and moral courage, which it is felt unreasonable to expect. But isn't that what people generally have assumed would take place after the war and a "democratic" victory? For obviously, unless a spirit of humility and repentance, a high spiritual imaginativeness and courage animate the victorious peoples; and unless the German and Japanese people feel that they can trust us and are freed from fear and resentment and the inverted egoism of an inferiority complex—unless the world experiences a spiritual re-birth—there can be no good peace after this greatest and most destructive of all wars. We cannot believe there will be. But what shred of evidence is there that conditions at the end of a long war to the finish will be favorable for such a re-birth, more than conditions today? Is it not rather that, every day the war drags on, fresh evidence appears that we have not the will nor the strength to "turn again and be saved"? And, when was the law repealed which warns men, even as it woos their spirits—"Now is the accepted time; now is the day of salvation"?

If we do not wait until the spiritual energies of this generation are utterly exhausted to offer proposals for a creative peace we may yet find salvation. It may not seem likely, but when we think of the deep-seated reluctance in the hearts of all peoples to go to war, the inability of all the modern machinery of propaganda to arouse any enthusiasm for war in their breasts, it is not impossible that one of these days the utter futility and irrationality of it might seize upon millions, that they would lay down their arms, and walk home. When we remember with what joy the masses, in 1917-18, hailed the bright promise which was held out by President Wilson's Fourteen Points, and by the Russian Revolution in its early idealistic days, there is a possibility that there would be a tremendous, spontaneous response to such dynamic peace action by the United States which could not be ignored. Why, in any event, should so many Christians be so sure that the way of reconciliation would not work?

Even as these words were being written, the fall of Manila, Singapore, Rangoon, Sumatra, Java stunned the Western world. With fearful dispatch an end has been made to white supremacy in the Orient. Whatever the future course of the war, that has been settled. These developments cause many people to feel that, for the time being, there is no basis left for any imaginative peace proposal by the United States. The Axis Powers, Japan in particular, would inevitably regard such a

move as a sign of weakness or even cowardice on our part. They feel
that world domination is in their grasp, after decades of defeat and
frustration, and nothing except crushing military defeat can keep them
now from driving on to the attainment of that prize.

If we are prepared to make proposals looking toward a genuine peace
only when we clearly have the upper hand, we cannot expect our national enemies to do otherwise. In that case there is nothing to do but
fight to the bitter end. It is now plain just how bitter that end will be.
If the full strength of the people of the United States, of the millions
and hundreds of millions of Russia, China, India, the Near East, South
America, as well as the desperate ultimate efforts of Great Britain, Germany, Italy and Japan are to be thrown into this war before an end is
made of it, the war must eventuate either in a stalemate of complete
exhaustion or in the "victory" of one group of embittered peoples over
another group of despairing peoples. Both will have been brutalized by
the most hideous warfare in all the tortured course of human history,
and both must dwell on a devastated planet of which it will indeed be
said that "the whole creation groaneth and travaileth in pain together."
This is not a goal for which human beings can fight rationally. Verily,
if there was ever an occasion when it seemed wise for adversaries to
agree quickly, this is it.

Nor is it utterly fantastic to suppose that, precisely now, when they
feel that the stigma of inferiority has to some extent been removed from
them and that they could negotiate as equals with equals, the Japanese
and the German people may be more willing and better able to discuss
a just peace than before. There is no evidence that they are intoxicated
with victory as nations sometimes have been. It is reasonable to suppose
that, whatever may be true of certain of their leaders, multitudes in
these as in other lands are well aware that the costs of prolonged conflict
will be incalculable. A chance to sit down together with other peoples
of the earth in friendship, and to work together at utilizing the earth's
resources and modern technology in order to build the good life for all,
offers them more than Hitler and the Japanese militarists—even if victorious—can bring to them. By offering them that chance we on our
part will gain more than a victory of the United States, Britain and their
allies can bring to us.

And if, finally, the nation and the world are not ready to try this way
and we pacifists find ourselves a minority which seems to have no immediate political influence, seems indeed to be quite irrelevant, to belong as it were to another world, what then? That will not alter our
course. As Howard H. Brinton has reminded us so effectively in his
recent contribution to the Pendle Hill Historical Studies, "Sources of

the Quaker Peace Testimony," our pacifism is not primarily that of objectors to war or of peace propagandists. We believe that there are rational and pragmatic arguments to support our pacifism; but it rests finally upon "arguments based on the direct insight of the soul into the nature of Truth and Goodness, an insight interpreted as a revelation through Divine Light and Life. According to this view, a certain way of life is intuitively recognized as good and war is seen to be incongruous. This argument is primary, because the Divine Light is not only the source of knowledge but the source of power. The Light shines deep within at the springs of the will." Wherefore, God helping us, we can do no other.

We are sustained indeed by the evidence which history affords that "the little fellowships of the holy imagination which keep alive in men sensitivity to moral issues" and faith in the Eternal Love may indeed be more effective than surface appearances indicate. Sometimes they may have been the carriers of the seed out of which sprang the harvests that have nourished nations and civilizations. If God's peaceable Kingdom is ever to come on earth, it must, as Isaac Penington wrote in 1661, "have a beginning before it can grow and be perfected. And where should it begin but in some particulars [individuals] in a nation and so spread by degrees? Therefore, whoever desires to see this lovely state brought forth in the general must cherish it in the particular."

Or, as one said many centuries earlier: "Ye are the salt of the earth; but if the salt have lost its savor, it is thenceforth good for nothing."

Yes, though we be driven still further "out of this world," into seeming futility, confined to very simple living in small cooperative groups and, for the rest, giving ourselves to silence, meditation, prayer, discipline of the mind and spirit, we shall hold to the way. The trouble with the world today is precisely that men have come to believe that "the only means which work are material ones, and the only goal attainable is material. The world as perceived by the untrained physical senses is reality and the way to master that reality is through physical force."

The result is that tremendous material energies are at our disposal, but our souls are empty and exhausted. Developing a consciousness of the reality of spiritual things and generating moral power are the supreme need of such a world. It may well be that now, as in other such crises, this cannot be done save through small groups of men and women who austerely renounce outward things, strip down to the bare essentials, and give themselves to the task of "purifying the springs of history which are within ourselves," and to "that secret labor by which those of a little faith raise, first of all in themselves, the level of mankind's spiritual energy."

There have been other minorities: for example, there was that party in Germany which had seven members when Hitler joined it a score of years ago, but which dared to aim at becoming the majority, and at wiping out all opposition so that there would never be a minority again; and there is that minority, of which we seek to be a part, to which the Word was and is spoken: "The Kingdom of God is at hand; repent and believe the good news. Go into all the world and preach the good news and make disciples of all the nations. Fear not, little flock. It is your Father's good pleasure to give unto you the kingdom. And lo, I am with you alway, even unto the end of the age. For God hath not given us a spirit of fearfulness, but of power and love and discipline."

The Essays of A. J. Muste.
Pages 261-278.

XIII

Hugh Baillie MacLean, 1909-1959

Coming to New Brunswick from Scotland, and teaching from 1948 until
his untimely death in 1959, Dr. MacLean was the center of controversy
on account of statements made in his here reprinted inaugural address,
statements which follow readily in the line of thought of such prede-
cessors as John De Witt and Ferdinand Schenck. Dr. MacLean is remembered by many of the present generation as a friendly, devout,
scholarly teacher and preacher, a powerful force for spiritual growth in
the seminary community.

The Relevance of the Old Testament

Mr. President of General Synod, Mr. President of New Brunswick Theological Seminary, distinguished guests, members of the Faculty, ministers and friends:

On an occasion such as this, as I think back over the names of those scholars and saints into whose labors I have now entered, through whose scholarship and saintly lives the pages of the Old Testament have been unravelled; as I think of the task to which you have called me—to help train young men for the Christian ministry; as I think of the blundering, selfish, suspicious world in which that ministry is to be exercised—a world that at times may seem to daunt the spirit even of the most courageous among us—I realize how much I, myself, stand in need of the redeeming grace of God. I realize something at least of the prophet Isaiah's feelings when in the first glad exuberance of his majestic vision of God he cried, "Here am I! send me",—a cry which ended on that note of despair, "How long, O Lord?" Or of Jeremiah's feelings when he uttered these words, "Ah, Lord God! I cannot speak, for I am only a youth". In all humility, as today I dedicate myself to the task to which you have called me, I would reecho the words of the hymn we have just sung, not only for myself, but for all God's spokesmen everywhere through the world: "God of the Prophets, bless the prophets' sons."

How does the Old Testament relate to life today? Surely no more pertinent question could be asked in an inaugural address by a Professor of Old Testament. It is particularly pertinent because of the attitude adopted towards the Old Testament by many people at the present time. Such people argue as follows: we believe that Jesus Christ is the full and complete revelation of God. In view of this complete revelation, therefore, vouchsafed in Jesus Christ, any previous revelation is out of date and valueless. It had merely a temporary significance for its own day. If such people really had the courage of their convictions, not only would they adopt toward the Old Testament a Marcionite attitude by politely ignoring it, as they do, but they would also demand its elimination from the Christian Bible—a step which they hesitate to take out of respect, so they tell us, for tradition. Such people fail completely to realize two essential truths—firstly, that there is in most of the teaching of the Bible, despite the differing viewpoints of the writers and the different levels of religious experience there represented, a fundamental unity. The Old Testament and the New Testament are one and indivisible. Nor is it an adequate defense of the Old Testament merely to uphold it on the ground that without it the New Testament cannot be fully understood. It is essential to grasp this fact—that the story of God's redemption of the world is contained in the Scriptures of the Old and New Testaments. That story, which is unique in history, began with man's first act of disobedience. Nor can we dismiss the Old Testament part of the story by representing it as allegory. For clearly it was history in the first place, and must be regarded as such. We watch the majestic drama slowly unfold in the pages of the Old Testament till it reaches its grand climax in the New Testament. And yet how deeply are the New Testament writers steeped in the life and the traditions of Israel! Secondly, that God does not reveal himself in a series of abstract formulas. He reveals His nature by His actions. The Old Testament does not tell us what God is like. It tells us what He has done. It shows us God revealing himself in history, in the lives and experiences of real men and women. If God at one time acted thus, may He not still be acting in such fashion? May He not still be revealing Himself in the events of our day and generation? I submit that just at this point the Old Testament is particularly relevant today as we seek to find an answer to the meaning of history.

To all thinking people the events of recent years, yes, and of the present day, must be profoundly disturbing and perplexing. Great new movements are taking place everywhere. Once again humanity is on the march. What do these tremendous upheavals among the peoples of the world mean? What is to be the end of it all? So often we are baffled and in complete despair. It is to just such a mood as ours, to a very similar kind of world situation, that the message of the Old Testament can speak effectively and forcefully. For it is at the very point when the outlook is blackest that the prophetic insight sees the purpose of God. Out of the maelstrom of war, with the nation in imminent danger of annihilation by competing world empires, the prophetic voice rings forth loud and clear, "God also is wise." "Woe to them that put their trust in horses and chariots!" Events are interpreted, not from the human point of view, but from the point of view of a God who is active in history, but who at the same time transcends history, whose will and purpose for the world must inevitably reach a triumphant conclusion. When Yahweh began to be the God of Israel, when He entered into a covenant relationship with the people of His choice, an event occurred which was fraught with destiny, not only for Israel, but for all mankind. Israel saw her history as the primary sphere in which and through which God's redeeming work was done. And her greatest prophets on the basis of past history regarded world events as a mighty historical drama which would end in the vindication of God's purpose and the establishment of His righteousness in the hearts of men. There is the great contribution of the prophets of Israel to the problem of the meaning of history. Their interpretation was supernatural. Personally, I see no way of avoiding the issue—fundamentally, that interpretation is true.

But let us go a step further. Why do we regard the Old Testament as out of date and irrelevant? First, because of the time factor. The events with which the Old Testament deals seem so remote from this twentieth century in which we are living. The scene is different—their setting is oriental. Conditions are different. Life and society are vastly different. What meaning can events that happened in Palestine thousands of years ago possibly have for me in the United States today? That, as I see it, is the main task of the teacher and expounder of the Old Testament—to make the Old Testament live so that men and women today can see themselves portrayed in its pages. The time factor is not an insurmountable barrier. Scenes of bygone days can be depicted so realistically on stage or screen that we can imagine ourselves transported back across the years and share in the experiences being enacted, so much so that they become part and parcel of ourselves. Any study of the Old Testament must start from the Sitz im Leben—the circumstances at the back of the events there described.

Much essential spade-work still has to be done in this sphere. The relevance of the various books of the Old Testament to present day situations and problems cannot be seen until we know first of all the concrete situations which form the background of the books, and the circumstances which gave rise to them. Otherwise, the Old Testament is unintelligible. The great advantage of a historical approach of this kind is that we are enabled to trace the sequence of events in which the writers saw God's hand at work and His purpose revealed. Our motive must be much more than merely critical. It must also be religious. It must have as its final goal—that we also may know God.

We see the significance of Old Testament story and history and prophecy against the background of the time to which they belong. From this starting-point we proceed to ask what was their purpose for their own time; and what is their significance for us today? Then we come to a realization of the great truths that in and through the events of these days God is still speaking to us and that these old stories are charged with an eternal significance which outlives the years, and that they are relevant to every land and every age. In the intimate character sketches of the Old Testament we see ourselves portrayed; we see the innermost thoughts and secrets of our own hearts laid bare. Who among us has not heard in imagination the denouncing voice of the prophet Nathan levelled at him, saying, "Thou art the man"? There is in these stories a sense of immediacy and of urgency. Read the story of Abraham and Isaac on Mount Moriah. Is your faith and mine of such a kind that in obedience to the command of God we are prepared to give up our dearest treasures? Read the story of that great dramatic scene on Mount Carmel with Elijah and the prophets of Baal involved in a life and death struggle to prove whether Yahweh or Baal was God. Parallel this with the struggle that is going on in our world today between secularism and Christianity. Read Joshua's great sermon calling for a decision—"Choose ye this day whom ye will serve." What is your choice and mine? Old Testament history and story become contemporary history and story as we re-live in our own lives the experiences of the men of old, as we fight their battles over again in our hearts, as like them we make our decision between the voices of the idols of our day, the militant, masterful paganism which seeks our loyalties, and the call of God. All through the Old Testament runs this conception of dramatic choices. How extraordinarily relevant is this for our world today! Read the Book of Job and see how well it expresses the very thoughts and feelings that arise in our hearts. Read the Old Testament from this point of view and see with what sledgehammer blows it drives home vital lessons to our hearts and consciences.

Secondly, because of the language barrier. I am well aware that at the present time a controversy is raging regarding the merits and demerits of teaching the Hebrew language in a theological curriculum. I plead for its retention in the program. For Hebrew is not just another language which the Seminary authorities demand of its students in order to obtain a B.D. degree. The whole purpose of our study of the Hebrew language, indeed of all Old Testament study, is in order that we may understand the religion. Now the idiom of a language, which can never be fully expressed in any translation, however good it may be, can only be understood by those who know the language. Thus, in order to understand the Hebrew idiom we learn the Hebrew language. One hears much loose talk today about "wasting three years wrestling with the intricacies of Hebrew grammar." As a matter of fact, here in this Seminary we spend but one semester teaching Hebrew grammar. The position to which I have been called is not the Professorship of Hebrew, but the Professorship of Old Testament Languages and Exegesis. This indicates clearly where this Seminary lays the stress in the Department of Old Testament. The study of Hebrew is a means to an end. That end is to understand the religion of the Old Testament. We teach Hebrew grammar in an endeavor to equip the student for the Christian ministry with a sufficient grasp of the fundamentals of the language to enable him to read Hebrew with a certain amount of proficiency. Then he is in a position to make use of the tools at his disposal. He is equipped for the task of understanding, even in some detail, the Hebrew mentality and frame of mind. Let me give but one illustration. What does, "I am that I am" in Exodus 3.14 mean? In answer to Moses' question, What is your name? God seems to be telling him to mind his own business. His reply is tantamount to saying, "I will not tell you who I am." Others interpret the "I am" as an indication of the eternity of God. I do not favor either of these interpretations. Professor Martin Buber has pointed out—what every student of the Hebrew language knows—that a Hebrew imperfect tense can be translated in English by a present, "I am" or a future, "I will be." Thus he translates here, "I will be what I will be." This seems to me to make excellent sense. In answer to Moses' query regarding his name what God says is this: "I have no specific name. But wherever you are, in whatever circumstances you find yourself, whatever you need, if you call upon me you will find me. I will reveal my nature in accordance with your needs and your capacity to understand." Is this not the message of the whole of the Old Testament? Is not this exactly how God revealed himself through patriarch, prophet, Psalmist and priest? Did He not in the fullness of time reveal himself completely in Jesus Christ, His incarnate Son? And is not our task still today to interpret the meaning of the nature of God and His plan and purpose for us in this twentieth century on the basis of all His previous revelations? We face a tense, anxious, questioning world. We are confronted at the moment by a generation of men and women who have lost faith in God, in themselves, in political and economic salvation, in spiritual values. To meet this need I plead for a well-trained ministry, a ministry that is rooted and grounded in the language and spirit and mentality of the Old Testament. Only in this way can the Old Testament regain its rightful place in our reverence and esteem. Only in this way can the implications of the Christian Gospel be made clear to our generation.

But let us constantly bear in mind that man is human and therefore fallible. Consequently his interpretation of God and of God's will and purpose may at times miss the mark. Being seen through human eyes they are colored by human personality and reflect a human viewpoint. This is the explanation of many of the so-called moral problems of the Old Testament. Wholesale and ruthless extermination of peoples is attributed by the writers to God's express command. Our minds and consciences today revolt at the wanton destruction attributed, for example, to Joshua in his conquest of the Promised Land. But the explanation lies in the date of these conquest narratives and the background against which they were written. As the Deuteronomic writers saw the picture at the end of the seventh century B.C., with the northern kingdom of Israel in exile and the southern kingdom of Judah threatened with imminent destruction, they concluded that the root cause was the secularization of life and religion through contact with the local inhabitants of Canaan. Thus they rewrote the history of Israel with this philosophy in mind. Nothing that stood in the way of fellowship of Yahweh must be permitted. This had been Yahweh's command to Moses, and had it been obeyed, everything would have been well. In this day and age in which we live, when secularization has cut deep into the very core of human life, is not this lesson grimly relevant? History may have been falsified in the interests of philosophy, but the moral lesson is still true. How often critics of the Old Testament tend to regard it as being on a flat inspirational level and argue as though throughout it had a constant spiritual value. It is almost unnecessary to say that there are many passages in the Old Testament which have no meaning for our world. There are doctrines which are outmoded and no longer valid, because they have been superseded by the revelation in Jesus Christ. It is just here that I see the great value of expository preaching from the Old Testament. For only as the book, the chapter, the verse, are seen in their true perspective, against the background of the times when they were written, will their relevance to human needs and aspirations be seen.

A good example of this is provided in the Book of Psalms. For long most of them were attributed to King David and were interpreted against the background of particular incidents in his life. This attempt had finally to be abandoned when it was shown that David could not have written some of the Psalms attributed to him. Efforts were then made to date the individual Psalms in an endeavor to see them in the setting to which they belonged. But these efforts also failed through lack of sufficient data in the Psalms themselves. A new era in the understanding of the Psalter began when Gunkel tried to classify the Psalms into Gattungen or "types." He set out to find the Sitz im Leben of each individual Psalm. The method established by Gunkel seems destined to hold the field. It has revealed how extraordinarily relevant the message of the Psalter is to every day and generation. Here, just as so often in our hymnaries, we find the deepest thoughts and longings and aspirations of the hearts of men and women expressed: "the hopes and fears of all the years." Conditions may vary, but the same old problems beset mankind; and in its need the soul turns God-ward. Hope and

despair; comfort and torment; passion and peace; anxious questioning
and eager expectancy; doubt and certainty—every note that still pos-
sesses the human heart is to be found there, across the centuries still
expressing our deepest feelings. Is it then any occasion for surprise that
the Christian Church cannot give up the Old Testament? Its relevance
from the devotional and inspirational angles, its ability to be used both
in private and in public worship, demand its retention in the Christian
Bible. If only they were more deeply steeped in the religious spirit of
the Old Testament, if only they were better acquainted with its message
and its profound insight into the heart of man, the average minister
today would not be so panicky about preparing sermons; the average
man or woman would face life with a sense of less frustration and a
deeper confidence and courage. Too often, I fear, the present tendency
is to lose oneself in the intricacies of philosophy or of theology, and on
this basis to imagine that one is getting somewhere. We forget the
religious angle. I do not mean to minimize the importance of philosophy
or theology. I am trying to indicate the contribution which Biblical study
has to make in these related fields. Against this prevalent attitude the
Old Testament acts as a very necessary corrective with its practical outlook on life.

You remember how it is told of Jesus that He went back beyond
Jordan to the place where John at the first baptised. Weary and worn,
weighed down by a sense of failure and frustration, He retraced His
steps to the scene of His baptism, there to find fresh inspiration and
renewed courage and faith. Once again, at this very point, the Old
Testament is supremely relevant for us today. For it is a reservoir of
religious experience vouchsafed in a unique way. In an age that is characterized by doubt and longing it carries us back across the centuries
to the source of our faith. It relates our Christian faith to the religious
experiences of Israel of old and shows us our place in the great religious
heritage to which we have fallen heir. Professor C. R. North tells how
he heard the late Dr. Claude Montefiori once testify to what a comfort
it was to him to turn from the intellectual perplexities of modern philosophy to the Old Testament, which seemed so utterly unaware of any
such perplexities. Was he just burying his head in the sand? I think not.
The Old Testament recalls us to the fact that no philosophy and no
theology can be satisfying to the soul of man which does not bring man
face to face with the living God and face to face with eternal realities.

Or think of the prophets of the Old Testament. For the most part
they were like voices crying in the wilderness, and their messages went
unheeded by their own countrymen. On occasion their prophecies were
unfulfilled, though uttered in the name of Yahweh. All too often they
appear as violently nationalistic, and utter prophecies of dire doom and

destruction upon their foes and upon the surrounding nations—all in
the name of Yahweh. Even among the prophecies of Second Isaiah—
that prince of Old Testament prophets—we find the same tendency.
Compare, for example, this quotation:

> Look unto Me, and be ye saved,
> all the ends of the earth;
> For I am God, and there is none else.
> By myself have I sworn,
> The word is gone from My mouth
> in righteousness, and shall not return,
> That unto Me every knee shall bow,
> Every tongue shall swear.
>
> Isaiah 45.22 sqq.

with this:

> Egypt I give as your ransom,
> Ethiopia and Seba in exchange for you;
> Because you are precious in my sight,
> Honored and loved by me,
> Lands I give in exchange for you.
>
> Isaiah 43.3 sqq

or this:

> . . . kings shall be your foster fathers,
> And their queens your nursing mothers:
> With their faces to the earth
> shall they bow down to you.
> And shall lick the dust of your feet.
>
> Isaiah 49.23

What relevance can such prophecies possibly have for today, you ask,
more especially in view of the cross of Calvary? But far from gloating
over our much vaunted progress; far from boasting about our Christian
spirit; far from maintaining the irrelevance of such sentiments; do we
not see how tragically relevant these very sentiments are to our world?
Do we not see that it is largely national pride and aggrandizement that
have involved our world in two major wars already? Do we not see that
far from approaching the Christian ethic and the ideal of Christ we are
still at the Old Testament level with all too often its misconceptions of
the true nature of God and its preconceptions of God's attitude toward
us as distinct from other nations? Need we be surprised at the nation-

alism in religion which runs through most of the Old Testament? How otherwise, one wonders, could it have survived at all in the face of constant and unrelenting attacks from paganism without a policy of "separation" being enforced? It is the crowning glory of Israel that this tender and infinitely precious treasure committed to it was jealously guarded and preserved through the centuries till it reached its full flowering in the Incarnation. Over and above and beyond the misconceptions of the Old Testament, which are due to the human instrument and reflect the frailties of the human personality, there stands a genuine word of God, of eternal and abiding significance. There is the great miracle of the Old Testament—the prophetic consciousness. "Thus saith Yahweh." I regard the Old Testament prophets as men called of God to proclaim His will; called of God and inspired by Him to declare a message which has eternal relevance for every age. The "I" of the prophetic oracle is not the prophet himself; it is Yahweh speaking through the prophet. Each prophet has his own individual characteristics as distinct from other prophets, but in each prophet we see reflected something of the mind and heart of God. This is true even of a prophecy like that of Nahum which because of its invective, its vindictiveness, and at times almost crudeness, seems to many people to have no place in the Christian Bible. The prophet gloats in passionate exultation over the destruction and the desolation of the bloody city, Nineveh:

> There is no healing for your wound;
> Your hurt is incurable.
> Everyone who shall hear the news about you,
> will clap his hands over you.
> For against whom has not your malice
> continually gone forth?
>
> Nahum 3.19

What place has this ode of hate and vengeance, you ask, in a revelation of grace? What are we to make of the picture of an angry and vindictive God here presented to us? Let me make one point clear. Nahum's anger was not a personal anger. Nineveh had outraged the conscience of mankind by her cruelties. To the champions of Yahwism, of which Israel was the incarnation and her prophets the spokesmen, Nineveh's offense against humanity was an offense against God. The social conscience of mankind had been outraged. Therefore the face of God must be against Nineveh. Is there room or not even in a revelation of grace for passionate indignation against acts which violate the deepest instincts of the human conscience, which are contrary to the laws both of God and man? Are we today to spend our energies in trying to placate and come to terms with the forces of evil in our world, while contending in a vague, indefinite, meaningless kind of way that God is love? Is this how Hosea, for example, reached his conviction about the hesedh, the loving kindness of God? No, that conviction came to his tortured soul as the result of a shattering personal experience through which he was brought close to God. Read the prophecies of Nahum against their background, and they become vibrant with life and meaning for our day and generation. Or again, in these days in which we live of international tension, characterized by political expediency rather than principle, let us reread the Book of Amos in order to recall to mind the basis upon which alone international morality can be firmly established. Or read Micah, the prophet of social righteousness, and see how relevant his message is to the problems of our own age, when a social consciousness is particularly strong. The messages of the Old Testament prophets were proclaimed in the midst of a ferment of great competing empires. Thus they have particular relevance for the present time. Note how the prophets met these successive crises in the history of this small, apparently insignificant people. Note also how as the prophetic movement reaches its grand climax the author of Isaiah 52:13-53:12—the Suffering Servant passage—looks forward to the time when God's righteous rule shall be established among the nations, though this result will be achieved only through the destruction of the servant, Israel. Will anyone deny the relevance of this message as a torn and bleeding world gropes blindly in the darkness seeking desperately for light and for guidance? Every generation needs its prophets—men who will fearlessly proclaim God's will and purpose and interpret them in the light of present-day life and its needs. We need the spirit of the Old Testament prophets; yet more we need their penetrating vision and insight. We need their nearness to the heart of God. We need their sense of humble consecration and devoted service.

One notices today a new kind of stress in Biblical study. Analysis is giving way to synthesis, and on all sides attempts are being made to integrate our approach to the Bible on the basis of our knowledge of the life which produced the various books. And this building-up process will go on. The result of this is that a change of emphasis has taken place. Now the stress is being laid, not so much upon the religious ideas and how they came to be developed, but upon the religious community which molded the ideas.

I had the pleasure of discussing this point during the summer with my old teacher and friend, Dr. Norman Porteous of New College, Edinburgh, particularly in connection with the Book of Deuteronomy.

So often this book is lightly dismissed as a series of laws—a law code
contained in a framework, which has no particular relevance for today.
But what was the background which produced this Book? If we are
right in equating it in large measure with the law book found in the
Temple in the reign of Josiah—a point of view which the vast majority
of Old Testament scholars accept—then its date is about 622-1 B.C. And
it was written with a specific purpose in view—to make clear to the
Israel of that day the meaning and the relevance for its life of its classic
past. There is a great truth here for our world, and we cannot shirk the
issue. The Christian Church has taken over the religious traditions of
Israel and claims to have made them her own. But how true is this?
Let us challenge the unfaith of our world with the essential message of
Deuteronomy—that in order to have a living religion we must re-ap-
propriate for ourselves our classic past. The covenant at Horeb-Sinai,
the whole idea of the Promised Land, the conception of a peculiar
people, the picture of the Church today as "the new Israel"—these
mean nothing at all to us unless we, ourselves, relive these experiences
in our own lives and make them our own. Biblical history must be
contemporary history before it can be saving history. If we would understand the implication of the work of Jesus Christ for our day and generation, we, too, must tread the paths trod by the Israelites of old and
enter into their experiences of covenant fellowship with God with all
that this involves—self-abnegation, self-denial, perhaps even martyrdom, in order that God's will may be done.

In the difficult days that lie ahead I see the Old Testament making
a larger and wider contribution than ever before to current theological
problems. In many ways it is a tragic story—the story of a nation called
to martyrdom that it might fulfill its mission in the purposes of God,
and act as God's instrument in bringing the whole world to a knowledge
of Him. But in the course of reflection on these experiences through
the centuries Israel came to a profound knowledge of the nature and
characteristics of the God who had chosen her—a knowledge which we
neglect at our peril if we are to face up resolutely and realistically to
the tensions and the complexities of our day. In particular, unless our
world can achieve a similar kind of social solidarity to that achieved by
Israel of old—a solidarity based on the recognition of the unity of God;
unless our world comes to a recognition of the overruling sovereignty
of God in every sphere of human life, then the divine judgment awaits
us. Let us turn back to the Old Testament; let us watch the majestic
drama as it slowly unfolds; let it speak to our hearts and consciences;
let it encourage us with new hope and new faith; let us watch its grand
climax in the life, death, and resurrection of Jesus Christ; let us follow

the history of the Christian community through the centuries; and then on bended knee let us thank God for the religious tradition which is our heritage today and pray in deep humility for grace and strength that we may be equal to our tasks, loyal to our past, and faithful to the God and Father of our Lord Jesus Christ.

In the course of a talk on his experiences under the Nazi regime in Germany a German pastor told a Scottish audience that in his church no meetings were allowed by the authorities except for the study of the Bible. By so doing they thought that they would effectively stop the influence of religion. But the attempt failed utterly. Driven back inwards upon the Bible it suddenly burst into new flame and meaning for the people. We need an experience of that kind today. Only then can the Old Testament really live for us. And that is exactly what we are trying to do—to recapture for ourselves in this day and generation the triumphant notes of the days of long ago, when the pioneers of the spirit blazed new trails of faith by which future generations might attain to full moral and spiritual growth.

XIV
Joseph R. Sizoo, 1885-1966

Dr. Sizoo, of the class of 1910, acquired his greatest fame as a preacher in Washington, D.C., in the New York Avenue Presbyterian Church, "The Church of the Presidents." He also enjoyed a distinguished pastorate in the old St. Nicholas Collegiate Church of New York City, and was president of New Brunswick Theological Seminary. From his many publications we reprint an excerpt from *Preaching Unashamed*, written while he was serving the seminary.

We Are Ambassadors

Let me begin by making, ever so briefly, this first observation. There is no substitute for preaching. We are to bear witness. There is in the Church a place for ceremony, pageantry, and ritual. One should not fear them where they can contribute to worship and the cultivation of reverence. There is room too for administration, technique, and organization. But in too many churches too much time is devoted just to keeping the wheels turning. Indeed, there are churches where one hears little beyond the rattling of ecclesiastical machinery. Now pageantry and organization and ritual have their place and may be helpful in bringing people face to face with God, but what this blundering world is seeking so desperately today is to look into the face of the man of God who has climbed the storm-swathed sides of Sinai saying, "Thus saith the Lord."

There is another deep conviction which has come to me through the years. There are certain things which a preacher must know. He must know his age—the times in which he lives, the world of which he is part, and the community in which his life is set. He must see and feel the tragedy and tears, the hopes and dreams, the dilemmas and disillusionments, the faith and the frustration of people. Again, the preacher must know his Book—the source of his power and inspiration, the Book through which man speaks to God and God speaks to man. Then, too, the preacher must know his gospel. He is called to be an ambassador and deliver from the King of kings a message to the people of earth. He did not make that message, neither can he change it, neither can he disregard it. He must be able to give an account of the faith that is in him, and heed again the last message of Peter, "Be ready always to give to every man that asketh you a reason of the hope that is in you."

But most of all the preacher must know himself. Words do not mean very much these days. If words could change mankind, this world would be paradise. But words that are divorced from example and life fall upon dead ears. It is the man in whom words are incarnated who has a message for our time. The way he speaks about religion must conform to the way he lives with religion. If there is no relation between what he says and what he is, a cynical world will only walk away with increasing cynicism.

Let me make a third observation. Indeed, it is the underlying cause

152

of the influence of the preacher. If we are to recover the importance of preaching and be worthy of those who have brought the Christian faith into being, there is one word which must come back into the preacher's day-by-day thinking. It is the word "compassion." We shall have little to say to the dilemmas and disillusionments of our age unless we approach them with a sense of divine concern. Among the Omaha Indians during the frontier times there was a strange custom. If an Indian left the bounds of the tribe and traveled for a little while within the areas of other tribes, on the night before he left home he would be compelled to sit with the chiefs of the tribe around the campfire. Just before the fire fell back into gray ash, he would be asked to stand, and there silhouetted against a dying flame, would be compelled to lift this prayer: "Great Spirit, help me never to judge another until I have walked two weeks in his moccasins." The true minister of Christ must learn to walk in other people's shoes. One of the ancient prophets wrote, "I sat where they sat." Of Moses it was recorded, "He went out unto his brethren, and looked on their burdens." We shall never recover the romance of preaching until there comes back this compassion.

That was the glory of the preaching ministry of Jesus. The most striking characteristic of his life was his approachableness. He identified himself with people. He shared with them their common lot. He became part of the life of his generation. He seemed to belong to them. Nothing that happened to people was foreign to him. He dragged the sorrows of his generation across his soul. He could not keep himself out of the welter and misery of men. Their problems were his problems, their dilemmas were his dilemmas, their pain was his anguish, their disappointments were his sorrow. At midnight it was a Hebrew scholar; at daybreak it was a foundering ship; at noonday it was a fallen girl at the well; in the afternoon it was a company of hungry unemployed. Across the threshold of his home in Capernaum there fell the shadows of the limping and the lame, the halt and the blind. And he healed them all. He identified himself with the paralytic who had just enough feeling to know pain. He became one with the lepers whose bodies writhed in anguish. He seemed to belong to the blind who stumbled through the streets of eternal darkness. He cared what happened to the lily that had faded, the reed that was bent, the coin that was lost, the prodigal who had stepped across the threshold of indiscretion. He was the most compassionate man who ever lived.

There were two things Jesus did not know how to do. He did not know how to doubt, and he did not know how to hate. To the end of the end he lived with a love that would not let man go and with a faith that would not let God go. He was touched by the feelings of man's infirmity. He was always taking a towel and girding himself.

There can never be great preaching without great compassion. It is so easy to live comfortable lives, wrap ourselves up in the dry ice of calloused unconcern. We are prone to climb into ivory towers, look at the heartache of the world, say, "What a mess," and pull down the curtain upon it all. One day Dostoyevsky wrote, "The only contribution which civilization has made is to increase man's capacity for pain." Unless we feel that pain and walk in that darkness with men, we can never hope to be worthy of the gospel we preach. Believe me, this blundering world is waiting for the sunrise of those men of God who see the sordid shambles, the pitiful disillusionments, the devastating injustices, and the dreadful cynicisms of the hour, not with callousness but with compassion; not with indifference but with interest.

I suppose the best known and most loved war correspondent of the last war was one familiarly known as Ernie Pyle. There is one sentence in the last dispatch which he sent before he left the European battle front. It is this: "The hurt has finally become too great. Hating this business as much as I do, one becomes part of it. You leave something of yourself when you leave it." He spoke to the heart of a nation about the war because he had a great heart. That is needed in preaching.

Do you know Emile Cammaerts, who wrote a little book entitled *Upon This Rock*? He was poet laureate of Belgium. During the war, news came one day that his son, who was a flyer in the R.A.F., had been killed. In that hour of sorrow he sat down with himself and tried to think through a philosophy that would sustain him. He wrote his conclusions in this little book, a prose poem. He discovered that his eldest daughter, the strongest and finest Christian in the family, was becoming very weak. He spoke to her about it and asked why it was that she who was the strongest in the faith should seem so desolate. She replied, "It is not a question of strength, it is a question of realization. I never realized before what the Cross meant—we are sharing the responsibility for that suffering now, and the crucifixion goes on." There you have the secret of all great preaching and the one element which is fundamental to the witness the preacher bears.

It is not easy to keep your compassion in a world such as this. You always have to fight for it. When I went to New York eleven years ago, I determined that whatever I would do or not do I would try to keep my compassion. It is hard to keep it in certain settings, but I hope I have not lost it. You never solve problems by calling people names. There is enough fault finding in the everyday life without the minister of religion joining the anvil chorus on Sunday.

The Protestant Witness

Protestantism affirms that our redemption comes not by way of good deeds, but by way of a self-surrendered life. The poignant search of all ages has been for some method of getting rid of sin. The eternal question which has cut through the unbroken centuries is, "What must I do to be saved?" Man is haunted by the sense of estrangement from God and his better self. He is aware that something has raised barriers which separate him from God. Some years ago a missionary was preaching to a group of outcasts in a village in South India. He used lantern slides to depict scenes and episodes in the life of Christ, which he would then explain. When he threw upon the white-washed mud wall the scene of the Crucifixion and explained its meaning, one of the outcasts walked up to the picture and called out, "Come down, Son of God; that is my place." That deep sense of guilt rests upon every human life, haunting him like a vice and following him like a shadow. The one thing above all other things he wants to know is how he can get rid of sin.

In the world in which Paul lived there was a cruel law for punishing transgressors. If a man was convicted of a crime and found guilty, the body of the murdered person was fastened to the back of the criminal with thongs and ropes. He could never take it off. He was never permitted to get rid of it. He was compelled to eat with it and sleep with it and live with it. He carried it about everywhere he went. Days and nights without end it remained strapped to his back, until the process of decomposition set in. It was a frightful punishment. One day Paul viewed this loathsome spectacle and said it was like that with sin, which made him cry out, "Oh wretched man that I am! who shall deliver me from the body of this death?" Yes, we all carry about with us this appalling sense of guilt. How can we get rid of it?

To all such, Protestantism calls out that our redemption comes not by way of good deeds but by way of self-surrendered life. It has caught up the watchcry which rings through the New Testament: "By grace are ye saved through faith; and that not of yourselves: it is the gift of God." The Protestant Church does not offer this redemption but proclaims it. It does not grant pardon; it bears witness to the assurance of pardon. It is not for the Church to give or to withhold this gift of God. Salvation is not vested in a self-perpetuating movement which assumes the right to give or to withhold it according to its own judgment. Redemption is not something which an institution can guarantee, nor is it something which we merit. Redemption is not something we earn but receive; it is not an achievement of man but a free gift of God. The barrier of sin which man has raised God has broken down through Christ. That is the meaning of salvation. God in his infinite love has offered to man a way out of his misery and frustration. This is the very heart of our evangel. It burns like a torch and shines like a star. It has proclaimed to all men everywhere the grace and goodness of God which we may expect through a self-surrendered will.

Protestantism affirms the oneness of all Christian believers. It is committed to keep the unity of spirit in the bond of peace. The Church is not a man-made structure; it is a fellowship of the twice-born. It is a comradeship of people who live with a sense of our oneness in Christ. It is held together by ties both human and divine. They share together the assurances and hopes of this common faith. Sometimes I fear too much has been made of this divisiveness in Protestantism. It is well to remember that most of the members of the Protestant Church are held together by very intimate ties of a common faith and hope. Indeed, 80 per cent of the Protestants in this country belong to six of the major portions of the Protestant Church.

And yet, let us affirm that its emphasis is not upon uniformity but unity. There is a vast difference between uniformity and unity. When the Catholic speaks of the oneness of the Church, he means uniformity. That is something external; it lies on the surface; it is a matter of outward patterns; it concerns itself with technique and regulations and institutions. But when the Protestant speaks of the oneness of the Church he is thinking of unity. That is something beneath the surface; it is a matter of heart and spirit; it rests not upon institutions but upon character. The oneness which we seek comes not through institutions but through a child-like trust and self-surrender.

This kind of unity, therefore, allows for diversity, and is much more genuine and vital than that which is enforced by external authority. Protestantism affirms a belief in the oneness of all Christian believers amid diversity. You have that in the world of nature. Nature, of course, is one. But nature is not the same. There is a vast difference between snowflakes and star clusters and rainbows and apple blossoms and tumbling tides. They are not alike, and yet nature is one. It is unity with diversity. You meet that also in human nature. Human nature is one, but people are different. Some are black; some are white; some are tall; some are short; some are red; some are yellow. People are different, but human nature is one. You have unity with diversity.

So it is in the Christian Church. We are one in Christ. But this too permits differing patterns. It is a good thing for an Episcopalian Church to have a Methodist Church near by to keep its heart warm. It does a Congregationalist good to come in touch with a Calvinist who has developed an organized system of belief. I would rather live in a New England village with its three churches on the green, each giving friendly welcome to one and all, than to live in some village in Italy or Spain with its one church which may be utterly unconcerned or crassly indifferent to what happens to people. To us the Church is a fellowship of people who live a certain way of life. It is a comradeship with God and with man. It is a fellowship of people who are conscious of sin, seek forgiveness, and have found the grace of God in Christ. It is not an institution which is in the keeping of select and self-appointed groups; it is a fellowship of people, lay as well as clergy, in which all have a place and a meaning.

This, then, is the reason of the faith that is in us. Into this heritage, by the grace of God, we have entered, and we shall bear witness to it unashamed and unafraid. There may be other roads which lead to him, but for us this is a satisfying road. It is a costly road to travel. Believe me, great testings lie in the tomorrow of our lives. This is one of those either-or times, in which man cannot stand with his tongue in his cheek. Those who brought it into being were willing to pay the price. "These are they which came out of great tribulation, and have washed their robes and made them white in the blood of the lamb." This faith of our fathers to which we are committed is living still. We will be true to it to the end of the end. God make us worthy of the heritage which is ours. We may well commit ourselves to it anew in the words Bunyan wrote in his *Pilgrim's Progress* and with "stout countenances" say, "Set down my name, sir."

Preaching Unashamed.
Pages 21-25, 103-107.